Belonging

One Catholic's Journey

Frank J. Butler

ORBIS BOOKS
Maryknoll, New York 10545

Founded in 1970, Orbis Books endeavors to publish works that enlighten the mind, nourish the spirit, and challenge the conscience. The publishing arm of the Maryknoll Fathers and Brothers, Orbis seeks to explore the global dimensions of the Christian faith and mission, to invite dialogue with diverse cultures and religious traditions, and to serve the cause of reconciliation and peace. The books published reflect the views of their authors and do not represent the official position of the Maryknoll Society. To learn more about Orbis Books, please visit our website at www.orbisbooks.com.

Library of Congress Cataloging-in-Publication Data

Names: Butler, Francis J., author.
Title: Belonging : one Catholic's journey / Frank J. Butler.
Description: Maryknoll, New York : Orbis Books, 2020. | Includes
    bibliographical references and index. | Belonging is the memoir
    of a person of faith whose life journey brought him to the front
    lines and inner workings of Catholic Church leadership and the world
    of Catholic faith-related philanthropy
Identifiers: LCCN 2020006715 (print) | LCCN 2020006716 (ebook) |
    ISBN 9781626983830 (paperback) | ISBN 9781608338474 (ebook)
Subjects: LCSH: Butler, Francis J. | Catholics—Biography. | Foundations
    and Donors Interested in Catholic Activities, Inc.
Classification: LCC BX4705.B9838 A3 2020 (print) | LCC BX4705.B9838
    (ebook) | DDC 282.092 [B]—dc23
LC record available at https://lccn.loc.gov/2020006715
LC ebook record available at https://lccn.loc.gov/2020006716

To my beloved Fran,
who knows that belonging entails risk and daring.

*. . . take care and watch yourselves closely,
so as neither to forget the things that your eyes have seen
nor to let them slip from your mind all the days of your life;
make them known to your children and your children's children.*

—Deuteronomy 4:9

*What are those blue remembered hills,
What spires, what farms are those?
That is the land of lost content,
I see it shining plain
The happy highways where I went
And cannot come again.*

— *A Shropshire Lad*, XL, by A. E. Housman

*How baffling you are, oh Church, and yet how much I love you!
How you have made me suffer, and yet owe much to you!
. . . No, I cannot free myself from you, because I am you. . . . . .
And where should I go? To build another church?
But I could build one only with the same defects,
because they are mine, defects which I have inside myself.
What matters is the promise of Christ . . . and that is . . .
    the Holy Spirit.
Only the Holy Spirit is capable of building the Church
with such badly hewn stones as ourselves!*

—*The God Who Comes* by Carlo Carretto

Contents

Foreword: Learning to Belong, by James Martin, SJ   ix

Prologue   xv

Acknowledgments   xix

1   Uprooted   1

2   Be Ready for the Surprises of Life   10

3   The Arkansas Traveler   18

4   The Winds of Change   40

5   Call to Action   52

6   Growing FADICA   79

7   Everything under Control?   102

8   Fostering Transparency at the Vatican   112

9   Aid in a Time of Solidarity   120

10   A Dark History Revealed   129

11   Catholic Schools in America   144

12   A Deepening Faith   151

13   The Francis Revolution   160

14   Back to the Future   168

15   Joined as One Community   173

Index   177

Foreword

Learning to Belong

Frank Butler's remarkable life as a layperson working in circles of leadership within the Catholic Church offers the readers of *Belonging* an uplifting journey from the certainties and security of post–World War II Catholicism in the United States to the present day: a period during which members of nearly all faith communities struggle to maintain their trust and confidence in the institutional church.

I first met Frank Butler in October 2007, following the publication of a book on the lives of the saints. Frank had invited me to meet with the board of FADICA (Foundations and Donors Interested in Catholic Activities), a nonprofit association of grantmakers, when the group convened in Santa Fe, New Mexico, for one of FADICA's periodic retreats.

FADICA was gathering at a site that held great interest for me, as I am admirer of the writer Willa Cather. The setting was the former hacienda of Jean-Baptiste Lamy, the first archbishop of Santa Fe, who had arrived there in 1853. He is the lightly fictionalized protagonist in Cather's classic novel *Death Comes to the Archbishop*. Today the hacienda has been restored to a lodge with one of the most striking backdrops in the entire Southwest. I was delighted to have the opportunity to visit Santa Fe and to meet with Frank and the warm and welcoming laypeople making up FADICA, who were gathered to deepen their understanding of the Catholic Church, its charities, and its various spiritual traditions. I couldn't imagine meeting with a more impressive group of Catholic men and women, nor a group more dedicated to helping our church.

Frank was a major catalyst for FADICA, whose membership includes some of the largest private charitable foundations in the United States and Europe. Before taking on the role as its president, Frank was an influential staff member at the U.S. Conference of Catholic Bishops. He worked closely with the legendary Cardinal John Dearden of Detroit. Dearden, the first president of the National Conference of Catholic Bishops (NCCB), had been a driving force at the Second Vatican Council and led the drafting process for the council's decree on the role of Catholic laity. In the mid-1970s, when Frank came to work at the NCCB, Dearden was leading his fellow U.S. bishops in a celebration of the U.S. Bicentennial. Frank joined Dearden's team as his staff director and helped the bishops to craft the nationwide listening exercise known as the Call to Action program.

We have stayed in touch over the years, and I have gotten to know him and his lovely family. When Frank mentioned that he was working on a book, I became very interested in the project. I could imagine he would share some valuable perspectives on contemporary church history. But I also came to realize that his approach would hold wisdom for people who are hoping to see a more welcoming and accountable church in this current day of restoring trust in its leadership and institutional life.

I knew that Frank would offer a fascinating and upbeat story that would not gloss over the rough aspects, divisions, and scandals that we Catholics know only so well. His inspiring story is one of belonging to a faith community that has enriched his journey throughout his life and led him to places and events where his unique talents were most needed. Along the way, he has seen the human reality of a church up close—both its noble and heroic side as well as its flawed and even tragic moments of failure when fear dominated the decisions of church leaders.

At the outset of *Belonging*, Frank reflects on his lifelong journey as a cradle Catholic who is shaken by contemporary news of the breaches of trust and corruption at high levels of the church. He asks, as so many of us do today: How is it possible to reconcile a life of participation in a church that generates so many heart-breaking headlines?

Belonging takes the reader on a journey of remembrance through his cozy Catholic subculture of the mid-twentieth-century Catholic parish and school in northern Virginia, onto his life in Cocoa Beach, Florida, where his family relocated during the beginnings of the manned space program at Cape Canaveral.

We travel with him to a Catholic seminary in Little Rock, Arkansas, during the bourgeoning civil rights efforts of school integration and the horror of the assassination of the nation's first Catholic president, John F. Kennedy. We journey with him to a village in the mountains of Mexico as Frank and fellow seminarians live and work alongside its poor, learning lessons of compassion, hope, and joy amid hardship, and allowing Catholic social teaching to take root in him.

The story then moves us to Washington, DC, and the Catholic University of America during the time of the Vietnam War protests and the assassinations of Dr. Martin Luther King Jr. and Robert Kennedy, a time of volcanic conflict in our country. The author shares his struggles as he makes the decision to leave the seminary, pursue doctoral studies, marry, and start a family.

We accompany Frank through a period of explosive change and flux in civic and church life as he transitions from a job with the U.S. House of Representatives to become a member of the staff of the conference of bishops. We find ourselves in the heated drama of the hierarchy's first national effort to place justice at the center of parish and national Catholic life in the Call to Action bicentennial effort. We learn about fear and division within the hierarchy, but also about the courage and endurance of many rank-and-file faithful across the land who work for greater justice in society and within the church too.

The author then guides us to the fascinating world of Catholic wealth and philanthropy. We come to know the efforts of FADICA as its members create structures to support aging members of religious orders, to support the church in Eastern Europe after the fall of the Soviet Union, and to introduce management and financial reforms at the Vatican. And we see the clergy abuse crisis from the perspective of laypeople working for stronger structures of accountability.

Along this pilgrimage we gain valuable reminders of how Frank's connection to his faith and sense of belonging to the community help him deepen his own appreciation for the role all must play in keeping the church on the right path.

Belonging raises timely questions for today, when isolation is a growing epidemic among younger people—a generation missing in great percentages from America's houses of worship. The Pew Research Center reports that four in ten of the nation's 68 million millennials (ages twenty-three to thirty-eight) say they "never" attend religious services—a decline of 10 percent over the last decade. Not surprisingly, a third of that generation also report that they always or at least frequently experience loneliness—double that of the post–World War II boomer generation (YouGov, July 2019). Few dispute that a sense of belonging appears to be fading in America.

Young people today frequently describe themselves as "spiritual but not religious." By using the phrase, these young people meant they felt exempt from rules and dogmas or being part of what they thought to be an oppressive institution. But in stacking up the historical negatives and failings of Catholicism against its positives—including its core tradition of love, forgiveness, and charity, as well as the stunning examples of the saints and blessed—communities of faith come out on top.

"Not religious" can be another way of describing faith as something between only you and God, with no one to call you out when you might be off-track or to engage you in a life that stretches you beyond the comfort zone of self. It's a natural enough desire, but it also cuts oneself off from the wisdom of the community. In my experience, which has been shaped by the spirituality of St. Ignatius Loyola, founder of the Jesuit order, a faith community does not mean a loss of agency or freedom. As you will read in *Belonging*, it can mean just the opposite. Being part of a community of faith can lead to the shocking discovery of how much God gives us the freedom to thrive and the grace to live lives of goodness, generosity, and self-sacrifice, aided by those who accompany us.

This book is especially timely for a number of reasons, chief among them because it provides one layperson's front-row observations of the clerical halls of Catholicism at a time when Pope Francis has pinpointed the cultural divide between clergy and laity as a major area of concern. "Let us be clear about this," the pope said to fellow bishops during one of his many travels around the globe. "Laypersons are not our peons. . . . They don't have to parrot back whatever we say," he told the bishops of Latin America. "The sacramentality of the Church," Pope Francis said, "belongs to *all the faithful* people of God (cf. *Lumen Gentium*, 9–14), not only to the few chosen and enlightened" (January 16, 2018).

Frank Butler's engrossing account of what happened when the hierarchy invited the faithful to speak up during the Call to Action effort is a sobering reminder of how difficult it has been for laypersons to be heard within the church. It's also a riveting depiction of how clerical ambition looms large in the daily dynamics of a faith community.

Writer and social critic David Brooks has observed that now more than ever we need people who have the courage to live on the *edge of the inside*, who love their parties and organizations so much that they can critique them as a friend *from the inside* and dauntlessly insist that they live up to their truest selves.

The cogency of this story lies in just that: its vantage point from someone *belonging* to a community of faith. From that view we are rewarded by the loving and poignant perspective *from the inside* of a Christian grateful for his religious roots and for a church that journeys onward, learning from its failings and striving to become a more loving institution worthy of the trust of those who compose it. This is the view Frank now invites you to share.

James Martin, SJ, is a Jesuit priest, editor at large of *America*, consultor to the Vatican's Dicastery for Communication, and author of many books, including *Jesus: A Pilgrimage*, *The Jesuit Guide to (Almost) Everything*, and *My Life with the Saints*.

office within the church and not have had such monstrous behavior impede his ecclesiastical career?

We discussed the church's good-faith efforts in 2002 to put in place a zero-tolerance policy for clergy sexual abuse in dioceses and religious orders in the United States. We puzzled over the irony of reforms that did not address the behavior of the hierarchy itself.

Our pastor announced further "listening sessions" and suggested that parishioners make their feelings known to the archdiocese, to the papal nuncio, and to fellow parishioners. We all returned home unsettled but grateful for the pastor's forum.

The summer weeks passed, and in mid-August another explosion of church news centered on a report of the attorney general of Pennsylvania. It revealed seventy years of horror involving over 301 sexually predatory priests in that state and one thousand of their victims. The report showed how the crimes of clergy had been hidden by Catholic dioceses and how well-orchestrated moves by bishops in the 1970s through the 1990s enabled such clergy to continue victimizing children.

The public flew into a fury at the pattern of practices and seeming indifference of bishops. Never before had civil authorities so systematically revealed the internal policies of Catholic dioceses in the dark arts of covering up criminal behavior.

In a perfect storm of scandal, Pope Francis traveled to Ireland that same month to attend a World Assembly of Families, only to be confronted by hostile protests over the decades of abuse by clergy and religious in that country. Before Pope Francis departed Ireland, a scathing letter of a former Vatican nuncio to the United States, Archbishop Carlo Maria Viganò, accused the pope of allowing Cardinal McCarrick to function publicly despite alleged restrictions imposed by Francis's predecessor, Pope Benedict XVI. Viganò called for Francis to resign.

As journalists continued their extensive coverage of Viganò's claims, many Catholics, like me, were in a jumble of confusion and sadness. The Catholic Church meant everything to us. Like many Catholics I had been buffeted and had learned to accept the failures of the church throughout my life. In my career I had a ringside seat in the circles of church leadership. I had seen dark and disappointing aspects of its management. Even so, I was shaken to the core by the summer of 2018 and its revelations about an institution that was central to my life.

I lay awake at night remembering the church of my early years and the benevolent presence of priests at our family dinner table and their presence during important events of my family's mourning, particularly the early death of my father. I reminisced as images of my years in the seminary—peaceful, purposeful, and joyful—passed through my consciousness as so many gentle consolations. I thought back to the difficult decision to choose a church-related lay career rather than the priesthood, remembering how lucky I was to find myself working as a social policy advocate for the church in the nation's capital. I thought about the exciting decades of working with philanthropists united in their charity for greater impact on Catholic institutions.

In remembering these happier days, I searched my own conscience, asking myself what more I could have done in my lifetime to prevent the turmoil, scandal, and division that were besieging my beloved church. How could I have done a better job in living up to the high expectations of the Catholic heroes who lined the path of my blessed life?

In Steven Spielberg's award-winning film *Saving Private Ryan*, the main character, James Francis Ryan, visits the Normandy American Cemetery decades after being rescued by those upon whose tombs he now gazes. As he remembers their selfless heroism, Ryan whispers prayerfully, "I've lived my life the best I could and hope that was enough. I hope in your eyes I've earned what all of you have done for me."

I was now haunted by similar thoughts. The church was a place of high-minded champions in my youth. It was not the chamber of horrors described today in the daily news. This church was where I found extraordinary goodness, truth, and integrity, and where I learned that love, compassion, and service were the pillars of earthly existence. The church's wisdom and those whom I had encountered on life's path who reflected these values held the most venerable place in my memories.

Yet the grim realities of the present day gave me the uneasy feeling that I had missed something. *My head must have been buried in the sand*, I thought. *Was there something in the Catholic Church that I refused to see or acknowledge? In my long experience of working in Catholic institutions, had I been too idealistic and even naive?* Maybe.

I had seen the in-fighting, the refusal of church leaders to embrace the right path when confronted with an unjust administrative practice. I had witnessed petty careerism, church politics, mendacity, and venal preoccupations of clergy with wealth. I experienced close up the ideological divides within the hierarchy.

Still, despite all of this and even the latest news that stirs my anger, I remain left with hope and trust and a bone-deep conviction that Catholicism is doing more than any other institution to advance human dignity and freedom and to bring mercy and love where it is most needed. I have every expectation that the church will face its present problems, confess the grave misdeeds and injurious behavior of its leaders, and bring justice and accountability to bear on the harm it has done. I have this expectation not only because of the transformative powers of the Catholic Church so amply demonstrated through centuries, but also because of my lifelong interactions with this community of faith: my own experience of its immeasurable goodness along with its ignominious letdowns.

I invite readers to travel with me now as I take you through my own journey in Catholicism. Perhaps my story will help you understand why I remain hopeful and aid you in sorting out the conflicting feelings so many of us share.

Acknowledgments

Books do not see publication without the encouragement and practical assistance of networks of good friends and experienced professionals.

After turning the chapter in running a philanthropic organization for over three decades, my lunch with a friend, Fr. Tom Reese, SJ, sparked the idea for this present work, *Belonging*.

I talked with Tom about his own formidable success as a published author and editor. I then asked him about the merits of my writing an analytical book on wealth and contemporary Catholicism. While Tom said such a book might be worth doing, like the good Jesuit he is, Tom suggested an alternative: a book dealing with my lived experience at ringside with the worlds of the hierarchy and Catholic donors might be of greater value in this time when many are barely hanging in there after a steady stream of headlines about church leadership failures.

The book turned out to be highly shaped by Tom's advice and is reflective of a graced and, at times, vexing experience of belonging to the Catholic Church during decades of rapid change.

I am most grateful to Tom Reese for his welcomed and influential guidance.

Another star in the Jesuit constellation of writers, Jim Martin, SJ, encouraged me throughout the process of writing. Fr. Martin, an editor at large at America Media and an astute observer of things Catholic, not only helped me connect with the magical editing talent in Vinita Wright, but assisted me in practical ways in writing this book.

Longtime friend and former *Wall Street Journal* reporter John Fialka opened a door for me at Goldfarb Associates, and I express

deepest thanks to him. This led to working with the gifted Gerrie Sturman who believed in the project of *Belonging* and never let my spirits flag in our quest to find just the right publisher at Orbis Books.

Sr. Katarina Schuth, OSF, another gemstone in my treasure of friends, as well as being an amazing researcher and trend spotter within Catholicism, made many practical suggestions for the book and spent generous time reading the initial manuscript.

Jerry Filteau, an award-winning reporter in the world of Catholicism, also read the initial manuscript. His wisdom of years in covering the church and the bishops proved invaluable.

Numerous phone conversations with Dr. Jim Drane of Edinboro University transported me to my years at St. John's Seminary in Arkansas where he once taught me. He made the memories come alive for this book. His outstanding contribution to the Catholic Church and his heroism in the face of injustice will forever place him in my pantheon of great people.

I thank columnist and political commentator E. J. Dionne. E. J.'s warm encouragement to me to tell a story about how Catholic social teaching shaped my course in life was just the spark needed to keep me motivated.

To Paul McMahon of Orbis, whose brilliant editing gifts brought just the right touch to the manuscript to make its prose sing, I extend heartfelt gratitude both to him and his talented publishing and marketing team.

To my dear wife, Fran, who allowed me to bring her into the book, I heartily express the thanks for the grace of your practical help and ideas, but most of all for the inspiration and prayers to invest long hours needed to complete *Belonging*.

Special gratitude to my beloved family for their love and encouragement, especially John and Kate for their careful reading of the manuscript and their suggestions and "wows" that made me smile.

Blessings on everyone.

1

Uprooted

It wasn't our usual dinner in the garden apartment where we lived in Alexandria in 1953. Our dad was working at the Pentagon for the Military Air Transport Service as a civilian expert in the emerging field of airfreight transportation. He usually arrived home late. But uncharacteristically this evening, he was present for the family meal.

Usually, my mom, a nurse who worked at night, would dine with us four boys in the late afternoon so that we could do our homework and then deliver the *Alexandria Gazette* throughout Parkfairfax, a sprawling apartment complex in suburban Virginia where we lived. That schedule allowed us to catch a good night's sleep for the next seven-hour day at St. Rita's parochial school.

"Who likes oranges?" asked Dad as he entered the front door. My father was obsessed with oranges. His "good night" to us always included his somewhat enigmatic phrase, "May you dream of oranges."

Maybe his growing up above the cliffs of the stormy, freezing Lake Erie made him daydream about the bright, luscious, sun-drenched citrus groves of the tropics.

My father, Al, grew up in an era when the juicy pleasure of oranges was seasonal and an out-of-reach expense for most families. Whatever the reasons, my dad seemed fixated on the fruit.

"It's not even breakfast," said my six-year-old brother, Tom, as my dad hung up his hat and overcoat and took a seat at the dining room table.

1

"Well," said Dad, "pretty soon you guys are going to be able to pick as many oranges as you can handle." Then he paused and turned to announce to all, including our mom in the kitchen, "We're moving to Florida!"

Total silence. Not a peep from any of us. We just stared off in the distance, figuring that dad had had one can too many of Ballantine Ale after work. Perhaps he was just giving voice to his strange fantasy of living in an orange grove.

Mom broke the silence. "I thought we were going to wait with that?" Dad just smiled, then said after a pause, "You'll like it, Jean. You won't have to wear shoes anymore."

We all slept fitfully that night. At breakfast, my twin brothers, Tom and Dick, stared mournfully at their cereal bowls as my older brother, Al, finished his homework beside me while chewing on a piece of toast.

"You'll make new friends there, just like I did when we came to this country," Mom said from the kitchen. She was reminding us of her roots in Scotland, which she had left as a small girl, ending up in rural Ohio because of her father's escape from British authorities. He had been a captain in the IRA—the Irish Republican Army—during the Irish War of Independence from 1919 to 1921.

We were still quiet and already grieving the loss of playmates. Just two years earlier, we had moved a mile or so into our Martha Custis Drive address to find more room in a larger, two-story apartment for the growing family of six.

Al and I had already been through a sad separation from our schoolmates at Blessed Sacrament Parish and a rocky adjustment in our new parish school, St. Rita's, nearby.

Suddenly, we had to think about another move, this time a thousand miles from what we already considered our new home. It could have been ten times that distance, judging from the dazed and disappointed eyes of my brothers.

No more long walks to school throwing snowballs at each other, I thought. No more Sunday mornings at our parish. No more *Texaco Star Theatre* on our Dumont TV or the calming voice of Bishop Sheen, for Dad had also informed us that TV reception at our Florida

destination was nonexistent. We were abandoning our village, the friendly world we knew. At that age, if we could have put words to our feelings, it was the sadness of a farewell to a community and a sense of belonging.

Where we lived mattered. A neighborhood created an inner harmony in that pre-interstate-highways period of America. Parish Catholicism defined you at the deepest levels of self-awareness.

In Cleveland, where both my mother's and father's parents lived, your neighborhood and your parish said everything about you. Dad was from Lakewood, environs of Irish middle-class striving.

If you followed the local custom, you would start school at St. Edwards, move on to St. Ignatius High School and then to Notre Dame, the well-worn path that my dad had followed.

People had their favorite pub in Cleveland. These were ethnic enclaves where humor and scorn for anyone different from your tribe was part of the daily palaver.

Mom's folks lived in nearby Rocky River, slightly more blue-collar. The area was filled with trade union families—autoworkers, construction, and railroad men—who were just then beginning to enjoy the benefits of a healthy, expanding postwar economy.

My maternal grandparents could look out their front porch and gaze upon a well-built stone church, St. Pat's, across the street on Rocky River Drive. A new Chevy was displayed on the church's flanks aside Puritas Avenue for what seemed like a perpetual parish raffle. I am sure that someone actually won the prize of a new car, but we just never saw the vehicle move.

Our own St. Rita's in nearby Arlandria—a neighborhood between Arlington and Alexandria, Virginia—was similar in many ways. Though new, it was underbuilt in an era when few had anticipated the post–World War II prosperity drawing more Catholics to the suburbs of the nation's capital.

Masses at local parishes had been bursting at the seams since the return of GIs in 1945. Not infrequently, people waited hours in lines on Saturday to have their confession heard. Almost all Catholic schools—and St. Rita's was no exception—had long waiting lists for their classes.

America, historically unwelcoming to the endless stream of lower-class immigrants arriving at its shores, seemed to be changing its mind about Catholics in the post–World War II era. Old nativists took notice of Catholic service, patriotism, and generosity in two world wars.

Uncles on both sides of the family were back from Europe, and stories of their survival and heroism provided us with extra measures of self-confidence. Returning veterans also undoubtedly accounted for the surge in enrollments into colleges and universities as thousands exited the military to take advantage of the GI Bill. In fact, my uncle Frank was still dealing with injuries suffered from his service in the 101st Airborne during the Battle of the Bulge. Though serious, these wounds of war did not stop him from starting a family and entering night school while holding a day job as a marketing researcher.

The superpower contest heating up between America and the Soviet Union in this postwar America favored the emergence of U.S. Catholics from their once isolated neighborhoods. Proud of their war service and schooled by their church on the evils of godless communism, Catholics were viewed as valuable players in pushing back against the quest for world dominance by Soviet leaders.

Catholics of the 1950s were praying their rosaries for the conversion of Russia. Cardinal József Mindszenty of Hungary personified for the world the uncompromising Catholic opposition to communism. After torture and imprisonment, he had been granted political asylum in the U.S. embassy in Budapest and was almost as familiar to American Catholic school students as TV celebrity Bishop Fulton J. Sheen—a telegenic Catholic face whose Thursday night prime-time TV show captured huge national audiences and added to the pride of first- and second-generation Catholic immigrants.

Though meeting with ever-greater acceptance by other Americans, Catholics, for the most part, continued to live their daily lives in that subculture that was decades in the making.

Our Catholic schools and parishes were led by legions of

sisters often in anomalous garb with heavily starched habits and headgear that either squeezed the sisters' faces or blocked their peripheral view.

Big parish celebrations and street processions of uniformed parochial school children marched through sword-lined tunnels formed by plume-hatted Knights of Columbus, definitely a car-stopping scene. Catholics were, well, different.

Over decades, immigrant Catholics had established a network of fraternal and charitable associations providing the insulation that the clergy thought Catholics needed to maneuver through a world that had corrupting designs on them.

The clannish defensive culture that Catholics shared sheltered them and provided enormous security against what was considered a wider world of moral danger. Rules and roles within the fortress of U.S. Catholicism were clear. We even wore uniforms to school to highlight our group identity. All my brothers donned gray trousers, white shirts, and navy blue clip-on ties and trekked off to the schoolyard as an extension of home and the church.

Regular confession, Sunday Mass, celebrating first communions, and taking part in the Friday stations of the cross marked the weekly pace for many Catholic lives like the soothing ticking of a grandfather's clock. Our world was ordered and charming and, above all, protected.

That is why my father's announcement that we were moving to Florida seemed more impactful than just something about a new job. We were leaving our religious environs, going outside the fortress, so to speak, to an area of the country where there just were not that many Catholics.

We moped for weeks. As school let out that spring, the family packed up the Buick Roadmaster, and the moving van loaded our furniture. We headed south, designated even then as Bible country.

The nuns at St. Rita's wished us well in what they called "the missions."

Days later, we were awed by the orange groves lining the Indian River as we approached our new Florida home at Patrick Air Force Base, Florida. There was little population there to compare with Virginia. Sandy roads lined by gas stations, beer joints, and bait and tackle shacks told us that our new environment would be different from suburban Washington, DC.

The persistent heat, the ever-present mosquitoes, the rainy summer, and the disrepair of military housing made the transition traumatic for our thirty-five-year-old mother, Jean. At night, we could hear her sobbing in the kitchen of our small, no-frills cement-block airbase house.

Within a little over a decade she had moved from the glamour job of being an airline stewardess in the nation's capital to managing a growing family of four boys now in the most reduced of circumstances. A survivor of the Great Depression, Jean recognized hard luck. It seemed to be at her door once again.

On top of the challenge of our new surroundings, my parents soon discovered that my mother was expecting again. Against all odds, Al and Jean were to be parents of a second set of twins.

My mother's stress and relentless unhappiness seemed to propel Dad out the door most evenings. He'd eat dinner with us and then announce that he needed cigarettes—a polite fiction justifying a trip to the Beachcombers' Bar just outside the base gates in neighboring Cocoa Beach. The Beachcomber was a hangout priced for the military who patronized it. They could buy fishing tackle and bait, get their car fixed, or drink their day away in air-conditioned comfort.

But we managed without Dad's presence. Typically, we would arrive home from the base school by late afternoon and most days find Mom folding endless laundry, as my brothers and I dropped our books and school papers and then headed back out the door to play.

"You two have altar-boy practice," Mom had said this particular day. She pointed to me and my brother Al, often referred to as Alby, my lanky older brother, as he headed for the refrigerator. "Grab your bikes and get a move on it," Mom commanded.

Mom had signed the two of us up at the base chapel, and now we were memorizing a pamphlet by Father Charles Carmody, *Learning to Serve*. It introduced us to Latin phrases and demonstrated their pronunciation by providing sentences in English. We'd recite them to each other on our bike ride to the base chapel, pretending to be people from another country. "Ad Deum qui laetificat juventutem meam" would be met with "Deo gratias" from Alby, or sometimes a full-throated "Confiteor" shouted as fast as a tobacco auctioneer.

The base chapel was a sunny whitewashed building, more an interfaith center for prayer than the familiar church with cross and steeple. For kids like us, it was a playground inside.

We rolled the turnstile altar that accommodated the three major faiths that worshiped there and joked about what might happen if we were to rotate the platform during an actual worship service.

We gulped leftover altar wine and used the chaplain's typewriters and office machines to write comical notes like, "Okay, fess up! Who is hiding the golden calf?" And sign the note "Moses," leaving it on the chaplains' interfaith conference table for their Monday meeting.

The Catholic chaplain, Fr. Andy Mullen, CP, was a young Vincentian priest from New York who joined the Air Force for a brief period in his newly ordained life. He would serve as our pastor on the base, and have a huge influence on our family and on my future course in life.

Andy became a good family friend and frequent dinner guest. He eventually convinced my father, whose Sunday practice of the faith had been patchy, to return to confession after many years of spotty attendance.

It was always a mystery to me that my father, despite the piety of his parents and his extensive Catholic education, including four years at Notre Dame, resulted in what seemed to me a halfhearted attitude toward the faith. It terrified me more than I ever acknowledged to my father. I was once reminded by a priest in the confessional, after my father took me to a bar instead of church one Sunday, that if we kept up such practices all would be lost—leaving to an eight-year-old's vivid imagination what that might mean.

I had not yet come to appreciate the long and often complicated spiritual journey that most humans experience. At this time in his life, Dad, I guessed, saw the practice of his faith as regimentation. Was his example the normal youthful escape from rules? Who knew? All I cared about then was that somehow this priest friend of our family, Fr. Andy, had convinced my father to come back to the church, at least for a while. And that touched me deeply. For me, it meant safety for my father. But it also left a lasting impression of how the kindness and friendship of priests drew people back to the faith.

It was in these early days in Florida and from the life-giving example of Fr. Andy and others that I started to think about the priestly life. The friendship and warmth of this Vincentian priest were just the right things for our uprooted family coping with transition hardships and increasing household stress.

My father, Al, was the civilian cargo transportation manager for the airbase. He modernized the systems that brought supplies and material arriving at Patrick Air Force Base by airplanes, long-distance trucking, and even cargo barges. The oceanside base had been chosen by Pentagon planners as an ideal location for missile testing and, eventually, rocketry in nearby Cape Canaveral, five miles north of where we lived.

Because of Dad's position as the mover of all things on the base, Father Andy asked him to arrange Air Force transportation free of charge for all the Catholic children there to a Catholic school ten miles to the south of Patrick. In later days, this would have triggered an ACLU First Amendment challenge, but my dad's admiration for Fr. Andy and his decision to provide busing for Catholic students enabled Catholic military families as well as our own to fill up Our Lady of Lourdes Catholic School in Melbourne.

Each morning, dark blue Air Force buses with yellow stenciling would scurry through the northern and southern residential sections of the long military base, collect about a hundred children, and haul them miles through palmetto-covered dunes and pine-grove oases aside the Atlantic Ocean and then onto a narrow causeway traversing the Banana and Indian Rivers.

At Our Lady of Lourdes, the Adrian Dominican sisters taught

eight grades until mid-afternoon each school day, when the Air Force buses would return, pick up the students, and make the reverse journey, skirting the long empty beaches of the Atlantic.

The school's Catholic culture—with its First Friday observances, Christmas pageants, and uniformed students—reawakened the sense that we were reconnected with our tribe once again.

We looked forward to daily treks to the two-story school with motel-like outside passageways and stairwells. In the crowded but orderly classrooms, crucifixes, statues, and white-habited sisters with their attention-getting noise clickers made us feel loved and part of something larger, mysterious, and important. A simple joy about things Catholic coursed through my young veins.

2

Be Ready for the Surprises of Life

"Come on back," Alby signaled to Dad as he reversed our Ford station wagon and its boat trailer, creeping slowly down the concrete river ramp near our home on the Banana River.

All four boys stood aside as Dad freed the red wooden boat from the metal trailer. Then we impatiently urged him to pull the boat toward us so we could climb in.

"I want three of you to ride in the front," said Dad, supervising the logistics of our Saturday excursion. We were quite a load for the little Johnson 25-horsepower outboard that Dad quickly hand-cranked to a smoking and putting start.

We headed into the early morning mist on a glassy river behind the base. Brother Alby double-checked the ice in the Scotch Cooler, while my twin brothers and I sat near the boat's bow and took in the beauty of the water's satin surface.

We were going to explore the length of the river and maybe investigate a few of the small sand- and scrub-covered islands that dotted so many spots along the central channel of the inlet river.

Nothing was well planned; we even left our fishing gear back home. Just a father-and-sons venture like past country outings in Virginia, when we would often enjoy a ride in nature.

We could see the river's shallow bottom and the occasional stingray darting away from the noise of our boat as we scooted along the surface. A V-shaped formation of brown and gray pelicans flew between our boat and the shore as though these ever-present aviators wanted to serve as our official guides for the morning.

Whether it was the new parochial school, our involvement as altar boys, or the sheer natural beauty of the water, our feelings about moving to Florida were beginning to change.

What could be more wonderful than the trout leaping and splashing back into the sparkling water as the little red boat chugged along? We periodically locked eyes with our smiling father, who seemed very much at peace as he smoked a cigarette and turned up the throttle of the little outboard.

The water deepened, and we were now near the main channel that took boats and barges to the open Atlantic.

Within an hour or so, a hint of a storm was arriving from the west. We strained forward to see a distant causeway traversing our path when suddenly the boat felt as though it had descended a waterfall. A great churning rocked us from underneath.

A massive manatee, some twelve feet in length and weighing well over a thousand pounds, surfaced for air just ahead of the bow, and it felt as though the boat was going to be swamped by the huge churning and eddying brine that now surrounded us.

"Holy cow!" my brother Tom yelled as we pitched and twisted.

"What is that?" his twin brother Dick blurted out in panic. It seemed that the manatee had not decided whether to stick around and knock us completely to kingdom come.

But as the animal resurfaced, he just as quickly disappeared, and we turned to see our now soaked dad laughing uncontrollably.

"That's not a holy cow," he said. "That's a sea cow. They're harmless," he added reassuringly. We looked as if we had just come face-to-face with a monster.

Minutes later we could hear Dad shout above the motor noise. "Be ready for the surprises in life," sounding like a character out of Hemingway's novel *The Old Man and the Sea.*

Dad's playful comment would prove seriously prophetic in the months ahead.

The mysterious and sudden appearance of the manatee left us spooked on the way back to the boat-launching ramp. Thunder and darkening clouds descended over the Banana River. A sudden tropical downpour was on its way.

"Be ready for the surprises of life." That was certainly the lesson of our first nautical adventure in this place we were beginning to call home.

The months unfolded, and our lives began to take root with Little League baseball, paper routes, Scouting, and altar boy service. Many of our neighbors were Air Force officers, and they and their families were our swimming companions at the nearby Officers' Club.

Mom soon gave birth to identical twin girls. We were now a family of eight and feeling the tight confines of the three-bedroom, one-story cinder-block structure we called home. Despite the new sounds of crying infants, the arrival of twin sisters, Ann and Barbara, increased the sense of stability in our family. We didn't know, though, that more change was just around the corner.

In the early hours of an October Sunday morning a year and a half after my sisters' births, I awakened to hear Mom's panic-stricken voice calling my father's name.

Mom had been sleeping on a lounge beside my baby sisters' crib in a room that muted the sounds of nightly feeding schedules from the rest of us in the household. When she awakened at dawn to feed the girls, she noticed the light still burning in the nearby bedroom where my father slept. She entered the room and found him lying lifeless on the floor.

He was only forty-one years old. His life was over, ended by a heart attack. We might have seen it coming. The breadwinner for a large family, a hefty asthmatic who smoked and often drank to excess, is considered by today's health-conscious world a person at high risk of early death. Then, however, we had no knowledge of such things. Not one of us could imagine that Dad would vanish from our young lives so swiftly and permanently.

Our young mother would have to make many decisions in a short time. Despite the shock and grief of the moment, urgent questions plagued her. Would she have to return to Virginia or to Cleveland, where her family and Dad's family might be willing to help? What kind of life could a widowed nurse provide for six children in the mid-1950s should she choose to stay? How could she still afford the tuition for our Catholic school? Could she even keep her family together? These concerns left Jean no time to consider her own loss and the deep pain and fear that invaded her life so suddenly.

Mom had survived the Great Depression and immigration from Scotland as a five-year-old and was no stranger to adversity and even terror. As a child, she had witnessed her house being searched by British soldiers. She had been a nurse in an emergency ward. She was used to making firm decisions quickly, and this moment required lightning-fast responses.

We were to remain in Florida. We would find a small house in nearby Cocoa Beach. And sadly, we would enroll in public school because of the financial realities of losing our family breadwinner.

Within weeks, we moved into a brightly painted cinder-block home amid palmetto and scrub brush. It wasn't much. The road in front was not paved, and there were few neighbors save for the cicadas, snakes, and an occasional rabbit. But we were only a few hundred yards from the Atlantic Ocean, and we could hear its booming waves breaking on the beach at all hours of the day and night. It was a small dwelling, all that Mom could afford, but it was the first home we ever owned, and we had reason to hope that things might improve.

Little did Jean realize that the little township of Cocoa Beach where we now lived would experience one of the most expansive periods in Florida's economy. The nation was just a few years away from the superpower race to the moon from nearby Cape Canaveral. This would bring thousands of new residents to the area. Those years immediately following Dad's death saw our one-stoplight town and its island beach culture evolve from the backwater town we knew when we first arrived to a cutting-edge technology center for America's space program.

But for now, we were uprooted from Our Lady of Lourdes School in Melbourne—a school we had come to love—and now attended public school on the mainland eight miles away. Our new classmates seemed not only appallingly behind in classroom skills, but also challenged by frequent absenteeism and disrespectful behavior—something we had not known in our nestlike Catholic school environment.

Our family's exodus from the airbase meant that we no longer belonged to a Catholic parish. An itinerant priest from the mainland would travel across the narrow causeways linked to our new location, Cocoa Beach, and gather a few families for Sunday Mass. We first met in the backroom of a restaurant, and later across the street from the restaurant in Jake's Bowling Alley, the only amusement in town.

We settled into this new life drastically transformed by my dad's sudden death. Our loss and sorrow intensified our family bonds and mutual dependence, and it pulled us all into family prayer led by Mom every night.

Public school was close to torture for me. Not only were we Yankee newbies, but classes were years behind what had been offered in our parochial schools. My brothers and I were bored and turned off by the profanity and low culture of our new schoolmates, who made our classrooms feel like reformatories.

My new homeroom teacher, the first male I had seen in such a role, walked the aisles between our desks holding a wooden paddle. Occasionally, he'd use it on a sleeping student. "Grab your ankles," he'd yell, as he wacked a kid's backside while the rest of the class cackled.

Despite threatening punishment, students remained uncontrollable. Some skipped school, and others boasted about their scrapes with the county sheriff.

Graffiti on the toilet stalls and school hallways reflected a coarse and unfamiliar world that was downright strange and frightening for this eleven-year-old.

As I rode the school bus daily to the mainland across the long causeway from Cocoa Beach, I'd look over the sea caps of the windblown winter tides of the Banana River and long for our family's lost life in Virginia where we were secure and happy within the borders of our familiar Catholic world.

Dad was gone forever, but his words on that boat excursion

over the same waters I now overlooked echoed on these daily treks: "Be ready for the surprises of life."

Within the year, our mother had decided to start up a preschool in the garage of our house. As a nurse back in Virginia, Jean had bartered tuition at our preschool in exchange for her checking students there for colds and minor ailments. Now she thought she'd try to develop a preschool herself.

The state of Florida provided no kindergarten or preschool services, and a huge public need remained unmet. Within a short time, our house on an unpaved street morphed into a little school with a dozen four- and five-year-olds painting at easels, cutting construction paper, and singing children's songs.

In time, Jean found herself reading all that she could find on preschool education and stumbled on the Italian educator and physician Maria Montessori. Our mother was captivated by Montessori's pioneering research on how young people learn.

Mom asked the local town librarian to order Montessori's books and devoured them as the six of us children slept away the nights. This passion led to summer classes and her certification as a Montessori teacher, a credential that allowed her preschool to stand out and to thrive.

Her deep grief and fear lifted as the enrollment of the school grew. The worry about mere survival subsided, and sparks of optimism were everywhere.

Then came the U.S. government announcement of ambitious plans for military and civilian exploration of outer space.

It was time to let go of the past. One night, I arrived home to find two priests whom Mom had invited to dinner. Fr. Reuter was the current military chaplain at Patrick Air Force Base, and Fr. Burns was an older missionary who had been visiting the base from his pastoral work in the Bahamas.

After a modest dinner of meatloaf and potatoes, Mom invited Fr. Burns to take Dad's suits and clothes with him as he returned to his mission.

"All of this will be put to good use," Fr. Burns said as he smiled and thanked everyone.

Mom stood up and went into our tiny kitchen to get her purse. She wrote a check payable to Fr. Burns for $250—all that she had been given by a dishonest town jeweler in return for a bag full of pure gold plates, porringers, spoons, and cups given to my father at birth by my grandfather's boss, a wealthy coal mine owner in Ohio.

In the cloudy confusion of moving to the new house, Jean fixated on my dad's gold gifts and resolved to have them melted down and made into a chalice for one of us boys should we decide to become a priest. *What a good memorial to their dad,* she thought.

The jeweler, sensing that he had a greenhorn in this thirty-nine-year-old widow, confiscated the gold, presented Jean instead with a cheap ciborium obtained from a mail-order catalog, and a check for $250: our first of many family lessons about the exploitative wolves of the world.

"Please take this too," Mom insisted as she passed the check to Fr. Burns.

Later we would learn that Fr. Burns used the donation to buy building materials for the construction of an outdoor privy for his tiny mission church.

"I'd give you the ciborium too," Mom said, after explaining the origin of the funds, "but one of my boys might be a priest someday, and I know I'd want to give it to them," she explained to the two guests.

The priests looked at one another and then turned to my older brother Alby. Fr. Burns shook his hand and said, "Son, it's a great life!" reinforcing my mother's not so subtle recruitment effort.

We all smiled politely in uneasy silence. Alby was the only one who knew what was stirring within me at the time and how much I was really interested in becoming a priest.

Later that night, after the visiting clergy had bid farewell and the family retired, I asked Alby, "What did you think when Fr. Burns suggested you'd make a good priest?"

"Well, I would," Alby mumbled after a long pause.

"Probably right." I sighed.

Off in the distance, the Atlantic thundered as waves hit the beach. Through the jalousie windows, the bright stars of the

Florida sky and a full moon cast shadows below the palm trees that gently lifted in a slight breeze. Mole crickets called softly to one another while I thought about the future and all its possibilities: a moon landing launched from near our town, an improved future for our wounded family, and maybe even an adventure for me to explore being a priest.

3

The Arkansas Traveler

The drive up to the end of North Tyler Street gave one the feeling of entering a small college campus. At the edge of an up-scale residential neighborhood sitting atop a mid-sized southern city, travelers entered a walled-in campus with three large brick buildings designed in Gothic Revival style of granite and brick on the periphery of a curbed, grass-covered elliptical circle. A one-way road connected every structure to one neatly groomed picture of order.

Approaching the oval, one could enjoy a vista of the meandering Arkansas River and distant cliffs that marked a distinctive bend in the river as it skirted the city of Little Rock.

There were few Catholics in Arkansas. That made the existence of St. John's Seminary all the more extraordinary. Here, in the middle of the Bible Belt, stood a Catholic enclave complete with a high school department, a college, and a four-year theologate, which had produced priests for the South for the past five decades. It was the largest Catholic seminary in the southern United States designated a home mission seminary by Pope Pius IX in 1934 and intended to generate priests for many dioceses ill equipped to cope with growing Catholic populations.

While the majority of the students at St. John's—some 170 semi-narians—came from homes in Arkansas and southwest Louisiana, Oklahoma, Missouri, southern Illinois, and eastern Texas, it was not uncommon to find many seminarians from my new home state, Florida. Many were from farm families, which made life interesting when they mixed with students coming to St. John's from the big immigrant enclaves of Boston, New York, and Philadelphia. Surfeited with vocations, many of these bigger cities sent their surplus seminarians to the missions. St. John's was a common choice.

St. John's grew out of the initiatives of the Little Rock diocese, whose early leadership, like so many rugged Catholic missioners on the frontier, grew their own clergy out of necessity and the pioneer habit of independent thinking.

Edward Fitzgerald, the second bishop of Little Rock, attended the First Vatican Council of 1869 to 1870 and was one of the few opposing votes as the council fathers formulated the doctrine of papal infallibility.

Rebellion seemed imbedded in the church's culture in Little Rock. It coursed through the classrooms and preaching, sowing seeds for questioning and controversies that would someday overtake the entire seminary.

St. John's Seminary, Little Rock, Arkansas

But I did not have a hint of that when I stepped off a Greyhound bus that early September morning in 1958, having traveled alone over nearly a thousand miles of flat and rolling farmland. St. John's, it seemed, was a port of peace, and I was very glad to see my new home for the next eight years. I was thirteen years old, and I thought I had reached manhood now that I had struck out on my own. I was proud of my independence.

I embraced the daily routine: gatherings for prayer five times per day, three square meals at regular times, six classes, sports and manual labor periods, and study halls—all neatly arranged in a rhythm that reassured this new teenager buffeted by uncertainty, dislocation, and parental loss.

The homesickness of my first year, though deeply painful because of the distance from my mother, brothers, and very young sisters, was a price I was willing to pay for the exciting things I was learning from highly motivated fellow students and priest faculty who were my new band of brothers.

They were from working-class families like mine. Their fathers were farmers, car salesmen, truck drivers, and factory workers. John Berry, a classmate from Texas, was from a family of nine kids whose father frequently visited St. John's on his monthly furniture sales trips through Arkansas.

Tom Kelley's father owned a local car dealership. Tom was from a family of eight kids. He spotted me during my first week at St. John's as someone who needed an upperclassman's welcome and a little coaching on seminary life.

"How come you're not wearing a cassock?" Tom asked as he held out his hand to shake mine.

"I don't have one yet." I said truthfully. Mom could not afford to buy one and told me to explain that to the seminary rector.

I still had most of the ten dollars I'd left home with and was not expecting any extra financial help for weeks to come because of our family's diminished resources. The cost of even the most basic cassock would have been three or four times what I had.

"Tell you what," Tom said. "You can have one of my old cassocks." He handed me a black cloth bundle with some holes evident in the fabric.

I beamed. "What a lifesaver," I said, shaking Tom's hand in gratitude. No longer would I be the odd man out, wearing a shirt and black tie to the daily functions. No need to explain my poverty to the rector as well.

Frank Butler as a first-year seminarian

I adjusted quickly to the new surroundings and the friendships of salt-of-the-earth classmates as well as to the classical curriculum that was the center of our lives: literature, mathematics, philosophy, history, and languages.

The quality of the education of the younger teacher priests assigned to St. John's was exceptional, often better than that of older faculties in many eastern U.S. seminaries with wealthier endowments than St. John's.

Our Latin teacher, Fr. James Drane, had been a student at the Gregorian University in Rome and Middlebury College and was soon to depart for doctoral studies at the University of Madrid. He conducted his classes in Latin and constructed, with the help of some ham radio wonks in the upper seminary, one of the first language laboratories in the state of Arkansas. We could listen to and play tape recordings in modern and ancient languages, which gave an enormous advantage to seminarians who someday would study overseas.

Because of my Spanish fluency, I was ready for summer mission work in Mexico when I reached eighteen. The language lab gave a leg up to these smart farm boys from places like Paragould, Arkansas; Enid, Oklahoma; Waxahachie, Texas; and Belleville, Illinois, who went on to live in Rome, Tubingen, Brussels, and Paris.

I wrote home as often as I could, but St. John's was beginning
to feel like a place where my mind and spirit could thrive. A special
sense of the place wove its way into my life. Decades later, the
valley views of the Arkansas River, remembrances of hikes into
the neighboring wilderness, winter scenes of evening study halls,
and early morning routines carrying out assigned chores come
back to me in moments of quiet reverie when the pace of my
later life makes me hungry for the stillness and peace I knew in
those early days on Tyler Street.

After living in tropical Florida, I loved the rotation of seasons
that I found in Arkansas. Save for rain of the fall hurricane season and an occasional January chill, Florida's more subtle cyclical
changes were hard to discern. My body thrived in the crisp fall
days, first snows, and the explosive burst of spring that my new
home offered.

The seasons were my clock. The light of the sun changed
with each quarter of the year and marked the passage of time. It
sealed into my senses something about the place forever so that
whenever the sun sets in certain seasons, evocative memories of
place and time come back to quiet me. The season's changeable
sky added great beauty to the woodlands, creeks, and hills surrounding our seminary.

In those first years, I rose from my bed long before the official
hour of chapel to sneak outside and trudge through the first snow
of the season. An indescribable sense of glee surged through me
as I made snow angels in the nearby fields, becoming thoroughly
soaked and frozen; a grin spanned my face as I looked up at the
lightly leaded color of nature's canopy.

This habit of enjoying the natural environment grew throughout the eight years that I lived at St. John's. Weekends were spent
hiking with classmates through the nearby gorges and cypress-
filled swampland in the valley below where the meandering and
muddy Arkansas River weaved its way to Little Rock and then to
the Mississippi.

I never tired of exploring the thickly forested hills—the home for maple, walnut, and tall sycamore trees whose leaves lighted up every year in fall splendor. Nor did I get enough of the rich rock formations, quiet creeks, and winding paths that I wore down regularly on weekend adventures.

For some, our regimented, clock-bound life might have seemed like a prison. But I prospered in its even pace. No wristwatch was required. Bells tolled at the appointed times to mark events of the day: chapel, meals, class, manual labor, even sports. We were told that the bells were the voice of God, which provided extra motivation for us to answer them, of course. But as a thirteen-year-old I could imagine the heavenly choirs gathered around.

I became an expert in all phases of maintenance because we were assigned tasks we would seldom, if ever, encounter at home: driving trucks to pick up the seminary's food, pulling tree stumps with a tractor, and buffing floors. I even learned how to build a wall out of native stone to divert streams that often flooded one of the seminary buildings.

Some assignments provided lessons in science. One of the duties entailed a seismograph that the seminary maintained for St. Louis University. It monitored the New Madrid Fault Line that ran just below our buildings. The fault, which once caused church bells to ring as far away as New York and Boston, had not erupted since the nineteenth century. Nevertheless, it was considered a sleeping giant. Our task was to maintain a seismometer burrowed into the basement foundation of the refectory. We sent its recordings to St. Louis University monthly, where a Jesuit and his graduate students would assess them.

I loved this esoteric assignment. It permitted me to leave our chapel gatherings five minutes before the other seminarians headed to daily meals. I marveled that someone had designed a machine that could monitor the tectonic movements below us and wondered how scientists could read the squiggly lines and unlock the mysteries of the ever-moving and hidden subterranean forces.

In the years I spent at St. John's, the earth's plates below shifted frequently. It reminded us that even the foundation of our lives is not as stable as we often imagine. I think about this today amid church scandals and political turmoil. The solid earth, just like our lives, is in constant, unpredictable motion due to the collisions and interactions beyond our daily perception.

Despite the cadence of our daily schedule, surprise and wonder also marked our schooling. The young and energetic faculty shook up our too comfortable understanding of the world.

In those days, Little Rock captured the nation's attention because of its resistance to school integration following the Supreme Court's decision in *Brown v. Board of Education,* which knocked down the separate-but-equal educational policies of America's school districts.

In December 1955, a year after *Brown,* Rosa Parks had sparked a bus boycott in Montgomery, Alabama, motivating the civil rights movement throughout the South.

In 1957, the year before I entered St. John's, nine black students who, with the help of the NAACP, registered to attend all-white Central High School in Little Rock, had to be accompanied by military troops as they entered classrooms there. Arkansas, led by its racist governor Orval Faubus, became a lightning rod in the South, representing segregationist efforts to block and slow down the school integration movement.

It was in that setting that young faculty members of St. John's went about their work as teachers of future priests, doing their utmost to disturb and challenge status quo thinking. They were clearly rabble-rousers and ahead of their own diocesan leaders in Arkansas, who continued to segregate parishes and Catholic institutions.

Every time I took a Greyhound bus home, I entered the segregated Little Rock terminal. When I rode a city bus in Little Rock, I observed only white people seated in the front half of the bus. It was this divided culture that our young mentoring faculty at St. John's urged us to see clearly and subsequently work to eradicate. These bright, socially aware young priests had our attention and opened our eyes.

One Tuesday afternoon in early November 1958, I was headed to the dentist in downtown Little Rock, a twenty-five-minute bus ride from the more affluent neighborhood of Pulaski Heights, where St. John's was situated.

A slightly built African American woman in her late sixties, wearing the uniform of a maid, boarded the crowded bus. I rose from my seat, smiled, and pointed to the empty seat I had just vacated.

A white woman nearby spoke so that everyone could hear.

"You can't be from around here," she noted, as I turned my head to catch a glimpse of this pale, overweight woman in her forties and realized, embarrassingly, that she was addressing me.

"I'm a student," I explained.

"Well, that school needs to teach you better, kid," she quickly quipped with an edgy snarl.

Holding on to the bus strap, I looked at my still-vacant seat while the maid moved past me to the rear of the bus. I could hear snickering near the driver and saw a woman behind him shake her head.

Racial tension was surfacing everywhere. We were encouraged to keep up with daily news despite a seminary policy of only two newspapers to share among all the seminarians. In classrooms and moments of leisure, listening to the radio kept us updated on growing civil rights controversies.

Fr. Drane, our Latin teacher, was driving golf balls on the seminary football field one weekend, while some of us sat on a downed tree behind him, providing him with unwanted advice whenever he shanked his ball to the left or right.

"Hey, Guillermo," Drane called out to the guy seated next to me, whose real name was Bill. Drane had a habit of calling you whatever came to mind, a habit he no doubt picked up in his working-class neighborhood of Chester, Pennsylvania, where finishing school etiquette was in short supply.

"What do you think it would be like if you couldn't eat at a lunch counter or at a restaurant up there in Greene County [Bill's home in north Arkansas] because of the color of your skin?"

Whack, went the driver as Drane hit his golf ball.

Not waiting for Bill's reply, Drane continued, "I can tell you what I would do, buddy. I would be a number-one, hell-raising, lunch-counter terror," he bellowed, as he sent another golf ball flying out of sight. *Bam*, the sound of his stroke reverberated against the nearby building.

Books like Ralph Ellison's *Invisible Man* began to show up in our seminary library. Dinner table conversations were about John Howard Griffin's amazing account of what happened when a white man darkened his skin tone to experience discrimination in bus rides throughout the South.

We viewed the film *To Kill a Mockingbird* in our neighborhood theatre, and during dinner table conversations, seminarians shared stories from their own towns about the violence and discrimination that African Americans suffered.

We felt that a new awareness was developing across the country. We felt grateful that our faculty was a force helping us to appreciate our own dull sensibilities and racial privilege.

But our comfortable, protected world of the seminary felt increasingly insular and disconnected to what was becoming a national scandal of widespread racial discrimination in our country.

The pace of change was picking up. Thanks to gifted and good young priests at St. John's, we wanted to be in the vanguard of social change.

Then came the assassination of President John Kennedy in 1963, my freshman year of college at St. John's.

Not only did we consider Kennedy a hero to the nation, but he was also a special source of pride for Catholics everywhere because his presidency symbolized the acceptance of our faith group. Since our early immigrant days, Catholics had been victims of discrimination and class ridicule.

As we heard the news from Dallas, classes for the day at St. John's were canceled and the seminarians were called to attend a special Mass at St. Andrew's Cathedral in Little Rock, six miles away.

Seminarians filled yellow cabs lining the school's oval-shaped inner road to take us on the twenty-minute trip downtown. We stared as in a daze, and few of us spoke as we wound our way in a long train of taxis.

About midway there, stopped at a red light, our T-shirted and tattooed cab driver flicked the stub of his cigarette out the window and broke the silence. "Well," the driver paused and snorted after spitting out the window, "he deserved it."

For a quick second, my classmate John, who happened to be from Dallas, looked as though he was about to pound the driver's head into the steering wheel. "Listen, you racist prick, if you had any teeth I'd be sorely tempted at this point to knock them down your throat," John blurted out.

The driver looked stunned. He cowered silently for the remainder of the ride, occasionally stealing a glance at John's tight face, fearing a sudden haymaker.

It was a simple reminder for us that Kennedy's support for civil rights and school integration placed him in the crosshairs of southern hatred. Racial prejudice and resentment bubbled below the surface of everyday life in Little Rock. Our driver's observation was a sobering sign of how social progress was provoking the world of poor white southerners.

Two years later would come the March on Selma and a crescendo of news about systemic efforts to prevent African Americans from exercising their rights to equality, liberty, and justice. What we were reading about and seeing told us that social attitudes would require from us, as future priests, both vocal courage and action that could have a steep cost. St. John's and its young, starstudded faculty were getting us ready to be outspoken critics and nonconformists. This included the ability to speak up against unjust practices within Catholicism as well.

One Easter vacation in southeast Louisiana, I attended Mass with several seminarians in the small French-speaking enclave of Erath, Louisiana. Canadian trappers and farmers of the eighteenth century had navigated down the Mississippi from Canada and settled in Erath and surrounding territories in what some considered little more than a massive swamp. Despite the unique culture that the French introduced into the Louisiana territory, settlers living there profited by and depended on a slave labor system.

The large African American population in Louisiana offered the church an opportunity for new converts. The territory counted itself as having more black Catholics than any other area of the newly settled American states in the North.

Our Lady of Lourdes Church in Erath exemplified how populations of white and black Catholics worshiped in the same church but in separate arrangements. When I visited it in the mid-1960s, the church maintained two entrances—one for each race—even as the nation was steeped in daily protest against discrimination. The legacy of Jim Crow was woven into the fabric of Catholic life and extended to its seminaries and convents as well.

My visit to Erath was educational, and thanks to the formation at St. John's, I was learning to see things in my own church differently and critically, a skill that would help me later as I saw the same type of discrimination against many other groups based on race and gender. I was restless and ready to do something about the unfairness and the stacked decks of social inequality that were all around me.

In the summer following the Kennedy assassination, I joined a small band of brother seminarians and headed for Morelia, Mexico, in a three-ton delivery truck filled with donated medicines and clothes. Eight of us would volunteer for two months in the small mountain village of San Miguel in the state of Michoacán, historically the home of the native Purépecha Empire—rivals of the ancient Aztecs.

Our work was part of an effort of colleges and universities across the United States to provide a taste of country-to-country service patterned after the new U.S. Peace Corps, inspired by President Kennedy.

St. John's seminarians volunteering to work in Mexico. Left to right: David Makeska, Tom Barre, Dale DeCastro, Frank Butler, Bill Cingolani, John Manchino, Larry Dessommes, and Terry Thompson

Our project in San Miguel del Monte was to help the village build a clean water system. The only source of village water until then was a nearby viaduct constructed by the Mexican government for the nearby city of Morelia, the state's capital. Villagers illegally tapped into the government's water system, which was a constant source of dysentery and other waterborne illness.

With the help of the villagers, we located a clean mountain spring a half mile above the village at an elevation that would allow us to pump water through rubber tubing down to the center of the village. The point of the St. John's project was to promote the health of the village while providing a town water basin where families could meet regularly with neighbors.

Our team of eight traveled from St. John's through the Mexican desert and down to the state of Michoacán, a weeklong journey. Each night, we camped on the roof of the truck and looked up at the astonishingly clear desert sky overhead with billions of bright stars sparkling in the desert air.

Our border crossing in south Texas was almost comical in those days of low security, a time before drug smuggling and human trafficking were considered major border issues.

We had a hand-painted picture of Our Lady of Guadalupe on the cargo area of the truck in the hope that it might influence Mexican border guards to refrain from confiscating the medicine and supplies we intended to bring to the villagers.

Our strategy worked. We smoked cigarettes with the guards, shared a few soft drinks, joked with them, and when we determined that we had enough rapport, bid them a farewell without any of them checking our load. They shouted, "Bienvenidos, padres," then blessed themselves, laughing to signal that we had fooled no one.

Many camping stops later, we approached San Miguel, driving through gorgeous steep mountain passages lined with lush vegetation, flowering plants, and small plots of cultivated soil. I was surprised by the breathtaking natural beauty beside the extremely poor haciendas of the village.

The joyful welcome by the villagers was robust, complete with fireworks, a serenade, and warm Coca-Cola.

San Miguel Church, whose vestibule became our home, had

few furnishings, but we managed to sleep comfortably when we threw our sleeping bags on the cool, dry mud floors.

As the weeks passed, we settled into our daily routines of manual labor, prayer, and cultivating new friendships among San Miguel's inhabitants. Villagers seemed grateful for the presence of these gringo missionaries who promised to bring a new supply of water.

Still a growing adolescent at eighteen, I was particularly conscious of food that summer, not only because of my age but also due to the shortage of things to eat in San Miguel. It was the first time I had ever dreamed of food. How these fathers, mothers, and children worked the fields lining the surrounding mountains all day on empty stomachs was one of the more startling lessons of the visit. My gnarling insides made even the jungle vegetation look appetizing.

When hunger seemed unbearable, the head of our project, a deacon, would break out a canned ham, which we would devour in the church in the late-night hours when the village was asleep. Our emotions were a mixture of relief and guilt, but the protein helped us endure the daily diet of corn and beans as we dug the Mexican clay and put together the new water system.

The natural setting of this mountain village was more vibrant than any artist could capture. After rising in the early morning, I would enter the little adobe church of San Miguel as the rising sun's radiance shot through its front door. Across the deep valley below the church, a chorus of roosters echoed the arrival of another day of peace and focused labor. I thanked God for this beauty and the people of the village with their simple ability to endure daily hardship. Most of all, I was grateful that my Catholic faith had led me to them and a new awareness and connection with the larger world beyond the United States' borders.

While we dug our way, yard by yard, from the mountain spring to the village below, we practiced our Spanish on the villagers who worked with us, many politely overlooking our mispronunciations of the newly acquired language while quietly suppressing chuckles or simply scratching their heads.

Over time, we got to know much about the families of San

Miguel and how close to the edge of life they lived. Few villagers were much older than thirty. Many had left to find their way to the United States either as braceros—temporary workers—or as undocumented farm workers. It was rare in San Miguel to survive to old age.

Campesinos in San Miguel repair a school between daily farming chores

One day, a group of women who knew that I had been appointed dispenser of the donated aspirin and first aid for the group—which made me, in their minds, like a doctor—asked me to help a young mother who was seriously ill.

Veronica and her husband, Alfonso, were the proud teenage parents of a newborn named Juanito. Veronica had contracted an infection following childbirth. My thermometer confirmed that she was running a very high temperature.

I rode horseback to a neighboring village to summon a team of American student nurses who were also volunteering for the summer. They agreed that Veronica would require antibiotics and hospitalization. We had no such medicine, so the nurses recommended that Veronica be taken to a private Protestant hospital in nearby Morelia. It was reputed to give much better care than the civil hospital, considered a dumping ground for the poor.

Quickly, Veronica and Alfonso were put aboard our truck, and we descended the mountain through winding muddy roads during a thunderous rainstorm that occurred almost at the same time each day. The truck bogged down at a creek about a mile from the village in a rapidly rising torrent.

Word was sent to American students in the nearby village of Jesus del Monte, who brought their Jeep to us. In a short time, Veronica and Alfonso were back on their way to Morelia in the students' Jeep, as we remained and struggled to free our truck from the rampaging creek.

Days later, we learned that Veronica and her husband had been dropped off at the civil hospital because students in the Jeep had heard that the local bishop had forbidden Catholics from patronizing the Protestant hospital.

A heartbreaking message arrived in our village that Veronica had succumbed to the infection. There were no antibiotics at the civil hospital. Now she was dead.

Veronica's newborn son, Juanito, was presented to a brokenhearted Alphonso when he arrived back home in San Miguel. His serape was soaked and his sandals covered in mud as he wept, quietly looking at his infant son.

Two of us from St. John's stood at the threshold of Alphonso's little house while he quietly shared his story. Veronica's body, he told us, had been left in a wooden coffin alongside the mountain creek a mile from the village because the water was too high for the ambulance to cross.

Covered with green military rain ponchos, two of us and some of the village men accompanied Alphonso in the dark, descending the mud-filled road, with flashlights piercing the now relentless rain.

The memory of the difficult trip back up the mountain with Veronica's coffin has stayed with me over the years. No words were exchanged among us. Only the sound of the trickling rain on Veronica's pine box and our ponchos broke the silence.

Small whimpers interrupted our cadence as the exhausted, grieving men approached the darkened village.

We buried Veronica the next day in San Miguel's cemetery. Within a week, her infant son, Juanito, was dead as well. We never determined why exactly. It probably was due to malnourishment. A day before, visiting nurses had discovered to their horror a village woman trying to force the baby to eat crushed frijoles. When asked why she did such a foolish thing, the woman explained that nursing the baby would have brought bad luck from the dying mother.

The images of death, illness, and loss that summer in San Miguel touched me deeply. They were lasting gifts in my young years that helped me break away from the comfortable world I had enjoyed before then. So was the lesson of following capricious instructions from a bishop to boycott a hospital that could have meant Veronica's survival. Sometimes hierarchical stupidity had deadly consequences.

We ended the summer with a fiesta, as the villagers seemed to be able to celebrate life despite its sadness. We gathered in the new village square where the mayor, who was also the village schoolteacher, cut a ribbon and turned the valve for the official opening of the new fountain we had created. The clean mountain spring water now flowed. It had been months well spent, I thought, as we prepared to return to St. John's. It was not much time to make a big difference, but sufficient time, nevertheless, to open my heart and see the beauty and resiliency of a small village bravely facing life's adversity.

On my return to St. John's, I quarried into my books with a new intensity. Seriousness enveloped my devotional life, and something unsettling worked its way into my worldview. I felt the tectonic plates shifting within me, the early stirrings of change to come.

That fall, after my return from Mexico, I remember writing a paper for a cosmology class. It was on the ecclesiastical trial of the astronomer Galileo, who had proposed a heliocentric theory based on his telescopic observations—a bold act in a world whose scientific outlook, up until then, had been controlled by the Catholic Church.

For this, Galileo was brought to trial by the Vatican's Holy Inquisition, found guilty of heresy, and confined to his house for the rest of his life.

Some centuries later, the Catholic Church would apologize

formally for this injustice, but to me, an eighteen-year-old, it was another source of an awakening about the church's abuse of power.

I was learning that the church that was teaching me so much about human compassion, suffering, and injustice also possessed a darker dimension.

Research for the paper troubled me, and an unease triggered new and nagging questions about my life's aim to become a priest. I was beginning to realize the fuller dimensions of what I would be getting into, including requirements to follow the dictates of higher authority, which included people of flawed character and motivation.

This was far more than an intellectual debate. About the time of my work on the Galileo paper, I watched a real-life example of unchecked authority within St. John's itself.

Fr. David Boileau, a young philosophy teacher, was brought before the student body by the seminary's rector, Msgr. James O'Connell, a Boston-born priest. As the six-feet-seven Boileau stood silently and humbly in the sanctuary of our chapel, the rector announced Boileau's immediate reassignment to a small rural parish. The disciplinary action, O'Connell explained, was necessary to teach him and all of us lessons in prudence and obedience.

Boileau and other younger members of the faculty had been engaging St. John's seminarians in too much "outside controversy," as O'Connell put it. Things came to a head when Boileau welcomed a California Episcopalian bishop, James Pike, onto our campus to lecture at the seminary while our rector was vacationing. We all knew that O'Connell had been absent and unreachable when the opportunity to welcome Pike to St. John's unexpectedly presented itself, so our sympathies rested with Boileau.

Pike reached large audiences on television and from pulpits with liberal sermons on racism, capital punishment, apartheid, farm worker exploitation, and even topics at odds with Catholic moral teaching. The invitation from Boileau was intended to be ecumenical in nature because of our friendship with Pike's Little Rock hosts, the Protestant clergy, and besides, the brilliant Boileau thought it would be good for all of us to hear from people who disagreed with the Catholic Church.

Pike, a former Catholic and opponent of Catholic teaching on birth control and abortion, was beyond the pale for the bishop of Little Rock, Albert Fletcher, and it was he who demanded an immediate reassignment of those responsible for Pike's seminary visit.

Boileau's humiliation left us all stunned. Our once lighthearted conversations at meals and on playing fields began to reflect a new hostility toward ecclesiastical authority.

As my college studies progressed, St. John's began a small academic experiment. A political science professor, Calvin Ledbetter, from the nearby Little Rock campus of the University of Arkansas, was invited to teach at the seminary.

Dr. Ledbetter was a graduate of the Woodrow Wilson Center at Princeton and Northwestern University. Although he was not a Catholic, Ledbetter was interested in accepting St. John's invitation to teach a course on contemporary American politics to our college class.

Ledbetter's approach was exciting. He avoided miring us down in dry theory by using student debates to throw us into the politics of the contemporary world. We not only had to research and read up on current issues before the nation, but Ledbetter, a former Army JAG (judge advocate general) attorney, taught us how to marshal our arguments like a prosecutor to drive home positions against the opposing team.

Although the conflict in Vietnam had been under way since the mid-1950s, Vietnam had yet to become a household name. Regular U.S. combat units had not even deployed until 1965. As topics go, Vietnam seemed an exotic one for debate when Dr. Ledbetter first proposed it.

My choice to serve on the debate side opposing the arms buildup in Vietnam had been arbitrary. But as required reading and the debate itself took place, I began to see the conflict in Vietnam in terms very different from the Cold War overlay the newspapers gave it.

The more I read, the more I began to understand Vietnam as a civil war with colonial roots. This was a pre–Pentagon Papers period, when most Americans accepted their government's position as an ongoing defender of freedom and the only major power to contain the worldwide march of communism. Most Americans accepted and supported that narrative.

Preparing for and taking part in this debate over several weeks at St. John's convinced me and most of those participating that there was much more to the Vietnam story: an assertion of freedom and sovereignty perhaps, a rebellion against a wealthy and corrupt puppet government created by superpowers and former colonial masters maybe. We were beginning to see a troubling picture of American deceit.

Our panel of opponents to the conflict took the winning debate prize. More important, our classroom victory caused me to pay more careful attention to American foreign policy and the continuing manipulation of public opinion on U.S. involvement in Vietnam.

Until then, none of us at St. John's appreciated how this small series of jungle encounters would soon shake the very foundations of our country, kill and wound so many of our age cohort, destroy confidence in our government, and divide our national life for decades to come. And yet, this small Catholic enclave at the foot of North Tyler Street, with its engagement of gifted visiting scholars, had lighted one more fire inside—this time about the misuse of the military and the manipulation of its citizenry.

The nation could look to the Catholic Church to help in this task. For instance, there was Cardinal Francis Spellman of New York, military vicar of the United States armed services and a staunch outspoken proponent of U.S. engagement in Vietnam. He addressed American troops there during Christmas 1966, urging them to the "defense, protection, and salvation not only of our country, but . . . of civilization itself." Anger simmered within as I realized how difficult it would be to keep silent in the face of bishops who seemed oblivious to historical fact and blind to the evil of war.

Studies consumed me in my final two years at St. John's. I read voraciously in literature and philosophy, the latter being my major. While the bulk of philosophy in a Catholic seminary was then dominated by Scholasticism, a treatment of philosophy drawing upon Plato and Aristotle and early figures in the church, our younger faculty, trained in Europe's best universities, exposed us to modern philosophical thought as well.

We dove into Rene Descartes, whose framework was much less tidy and more subjective than the reasoned, observed world presented by classic philosophy. We plumed the depth of contemporary thinkers—Søren Kierkegaard, Karl Jaspers, Gabriel Marcel, and Martin Heidegger—while we spent less time memorizing the dry, abstract disputations of classic Thomism.

Modern philosophers were asking us to consider for ourselves what it meant to live an "authentic" life, one in which we rose above the interpretations of mediating institutions and unquestioningly accepted conventional wisdom.

Armed with the insights of post-Enlightenment philosophy, we found that our own opinions and experience about existence were valuable. For the first time in my life, I felt that what I thought and observed actually mattered.

My grades soared. I was maintaining a four-point grade average. Seldom did I spend time away from the library or my room, where I read, wrote, and prepared for exams.

The intensity of my studies was noticed by higher-ups. During the middle of my senior year in college, a letter arrived one afternoon from my sponsoring Florida diocese. The archbishop there, Joseph Hurley, had been monitoring my academic achievements at the seminary, and in the letter he invited me to do graduate studies in theology at the Catholic University of America in Washington, DC, rather than remain at St. John's until ordination.

I remember folding up the letter and breathing deeply because the news seemed to force me to face deep-seated doubts about my longer-term destination.

I slipped the letter into my pocket and walked to a park bench overlooking the Arkansas River winding below in the distance in the afternoon sun.

After eight years, I had just learned that I was now to leave what had become a sort of home. Memories returned: long treks in the surrounding hills, hitchhiking to Texas with a classmate to celebrate Thanksgiving with his big family, the tragic drowning of an upperclassman in the Arkansas River below, washing dishes, digging out tree stumps, the time I won the *Guadete* Sunday sermon spoof, and seminary vocation day where we annually welcomed several hundred high school seniors and invited them to consider the priesthood.

I was moving on from a familiar, endearing place that had shaped my outlook on life; connected me to God in a deep, loving friendship; and awakened a restlessness and questioning that would not let go.

In truth, I had serious misgivings about the priesthood that I was considering as a life choice. Both the growing discomfort over the requirement of lifelong celibacy and the strict obedience asked of priests were troubling, if not insurmountable, obstacles to a life that I wanted to live with honesty and joy.

I was deeply bothered by the battling and unfair persecution of the activist priests at St. John's. These courageous troublemakers were my heroes, my guides. I revered their intellectual and personal integrity, and I resented their banishment from our classrooms. Unknown to me then was the fact that within the coming year the local bishop, Albert Fletcher, would close the entire seminary after fifty-six years, in an effort to rid himself of the dissent and social activism that St. John's was generating. After the closure, more than 170 seminarians were sent to Loyola University in New Orleans to complete their studies. The largest Catholic seminary in the South was summarily shuttered by episcopal fiat.

Nor did I have an inkling, that day on the bench overlooking the river, that seminaries would one day have to deal with the gravely serious problem of clergy sexual abuse—a crisis that reached public consciousness decades later. The issue was never discussed at St. John's, although individual seminarians were at times abruptly asked to leave with no explanation given to the rest of us. Sex was a topic to be discussed only in the language of classroom moral theology.

At that moment in time, I could not foresee the future of the church, nor could I even see my own. But I was conscious that I had many questions about becoming a priest.

In the mind of my mother, I was predestined for the clergy. Disappointing her was a chilling prospect, but I was finding it increasingly difficult to see myself making this lifelong commitment.

The wind picked up as I gazed over the valley below. I needed to make a difficult decision, and yet, relocation to Washington might bring greater clarity to my thinking.

This wonderful chapter of my young life was coming to a close. I was leaving a beloved community at the end of Tyler Street and would miss this rocky vista—a setting in the gossamer dreams of longing that have followed me throughout life. Whenever I conjure up this view, even now, I feel the gratitude of those moments and recall the mysterious sense of inner peace I felt as I watched red-tailed hawks circling in the brilliant Arkansas spring sky, thankful for these formative years, and yet unclear about the journey ahead.

4

The Winds of Change

The beach was colder than I had expected. I was staring up at the cloudless, crystal-blue sky above, as Fran peered through the beach grass to the nearby Atlantic. We were both some fifty yards from the sea, picnicking on the side of a sand dune, our shelter from the brisk November wind.

We sat next to each other, listening to the muffled crash of waves and the intermittent squeak of gulls coasting over our heads.

"Don't you just come alive in this salt sea air?" Fran remarked as she smiled and inhaled the wild breeze.

I reached for the remains of the picnic we had been sharing on Assateague Island, Maryland.

The island was a vast acreage of national parkland filled with estuaries and wildlife, including wild horses. It was about two hours' drive from my new home at Catholic University in Washington, DC, where I had met Fran the previous spring.

Within weeks of entering the Theological College (TC) the previous year at the Catholic University of America (CUA), I knew that it was time to leave the seminary. Some months later, I found myself in a new status, working on a professional degree in theology as a lay university student, living with two former seminarians who had left TC around the same time.

I had finally summoned the courage to bring this unwelcome news to my devout mother, who masked her disappointment by saying that she was not surprised. Yet she drifted away from me after that, and our relationship changed and she would remain somewhat remote for the rest of her years. These were among the collateral effects that I had feared in leaving the seminary. I had such respect for my mother and the courage and independence she had shown in the face of the adversity and loss that had visited her with Dad's early death. Still, it was not at all easy to watch how my choice had saddened her.

Now I moved down a different path. I felt new freedom and tranquility that comes after a good decision is made. Years later, I would learn from the Jesuits a word for this: consolation, a sign from God that one had made the right choice.

I met Fran in a picket line during a student strike at CUA over the firing of theology professor Fr. Charles Curran. As a result of the protest, Curran was rehired in an unprecedented reversal of the hierarchy's decision to push out the outspoken priest from the faculty.

Many years since, Fran and I have revisited that moment in time—a pushing back on injustice in the church. But we also remember it as one of the most remarkable personal encounters we ever experienced.

During the student and faculty picketing, among hundreds of fellow students, the two of us were strangers to each other, and yet we locked gazes for only a millisecond as the megaphoned voices, placards, and crowds roared around us. A feeling of something more than simple attraction came over both of us, but to this day neither of us has been able to capture in words the power of those moments. It was a beautiful and timeless epiphany, obviously planned by Providence.

And now, many months later, I was happily resting on the dunes of Assateague, listening to my new friend, Fran, share stories of her growing up in New England.

"We spent a good part of the summer on beaches like Misquamicut, Bonnet Shores, Narragansett, or Scarborough," she told me, as I tried to imagine little southern Rhode Island towns and long stretches of coastal waters. "I always associate the ocean with happy times," she added. "How about you?"

I quietly took in the scene of three children searching for sea shells in the distance. "I guess the ocean was part of our year-round life in Florida," I said, remembering the long daily trips along the coastline highway on my way to parochial school.

Fran described the rocky shoreline behind her parents' home overlooking the Narragansett Bay. There, massive waves broke against huge Ice Age boulders, she told me. She shared how much she loved to sit on the rocks looking out at these pounding New England breakers and wonder what life had in store for her.

Fran's long brown hair glistened as the burst of the wind lifted luxurious strands from her shoulders. Her pleasant voice and slight New England accent warmed every part of me. The scene felt joyfully exact as the sun-heated sand and Fran's smile combined in an unforgettable winsome moment.

I had found friendship in my new and uncertain circumstances, and I felt nothing but gratitude.

As we drove back to Washington in the early evening, Fran asked me about the weeks ahead and my plans for Thanksgiving break. When I told her that I would probably join relatives in Cleveland, she said that if plans changed, I'd be welcome to come to her home in Rhode Island, where her parents always hosted students from various parts of the world who couldn't go home for Thanksgiving. Fran's father worked as registrar at the University of Rhode Island.

"Those Cleveland plans just changed," I responded impulsively.

Her eyes smiled as she turned to me without a word, then playfully added, "Well, I'll get back to you."

We both burst out laughing.

Some weeks later, I was standing on the rocks of Narragansett with Fran and her dorm mate and close friend, Ann Markusen, a Minnesotan. The wind-tossed ocean coastal scenery below the home of Fran's parents left me without words and deeply happy. Fran's family could not have been more gracious and welcoming. I marveled at the similarities of Irish Catholic clans who seemed to celebrate comfortably in song, humor, and robust political arguments.

Fran and Frank alongside the Narragansett shore in 1967

After four happy days at the Farrells' seacoast home, I was back in Washington, returning to my studies as a lay theologian.

The Second Vatican Council had concluded just two years before. Many Catholics heard and responded to the council's invitation to play a more active role in the life of the church. There would be, I felt, a need for lay theology teachers as implementation of the council's objectives took hold.

The dean of the CUA School of Sacred Theology, Fr. Walter Schmitz, a Sulpician priest from Wisconsin, invited me into his office in the late morning of an approaching Yuletide, now many months following my departure from the seminary. He wanted me to drop by to talk about how things were going.

Schmitz welcomed me into his office, smiling as he extended his hand. "How's CUA's only lay theologian?"

It was the friendliest word I had heard from officialdom since my departure from the seminary. In those days, seminary dropouts were referred to as "*ex*-seminarians," and *ex* is the Latin prefix meaning "out of." It was an appropriate description for this period of my life. This "ex" term was meant to stick forever and contained a hint of social stigma in the close confines of the Catholic world. Upon your departure from seminary study, you might as well disappear. The clericalism that Pope Francis would later identify as a church pathology was not a term I used then, but nonetheless, the isolation and shunning that I felt from former seminary friends was a manifestation of this problem.

Despite the billing of seminaries as schools of vocational discernment, students in them were considered de facto already belonging to the ranks of the church's clergy. It didn't matter that ordination had not yet occurred. If they chose not to proceed to that stage, an invisible wall of censure arose. Continued friendships with former seminarians were discouraged. Within the seminaries that former seminarians had left, references to the "ex's" were deliberately avoided.

Compounding the isolation experienced by former seminarians was the psychological distancing within their families. The shunning that I faced from so many quarters was understandable, anticipated, and accepted as the painful price of the choice I had made.

These circumstances made Fr. Schmitz's encouraging welcome all the more impactful. It reinforced my decision to stay with graduate studies in theology and later led to my return to CUA to complete a doctorate degree.

But on this day, I learned from Fr. Schmitz that his counterpart at the University of San Francisco was finding some success in developing a master's degree program for laypeople interested in theology.

Father Albert Zabala, SJ, the dean of the University of San Francisco's Department of Theology, had been born into a family of wealth that traced its ancestors to land-granted Spanish gentry of eighteenth-century California. The Zabalas in the twentieth century were one of the largest single donors to USF and had established a large endowment there for theological studies.

As a Jesuit interested in the implementation of Vatican II's call for a more active Catholic laity, Fr. Zabala was pioneering a first-of-its-kind program that would further that goal. Parishes on the West Coast were clergy-starved, even in the late 1960s, with many of them staffed by priests imported from Ireland. They were beginning to hire laypeople as religious education directors, schoolteachers, and diocesan administrators. The USF program was built around this emerging market.

Within weeks of my visit to the CUA theology dean's office, Fr. Zabala responded to my letters of inquiry with an application to the master's degree program. USF offered me a full scholarship.

I couldn't believe the good news, but it had implications for my deepening friendship with Fran. We were now commuting to campus together, and during the weekends we would explore the sites within driving distance of Washington, DC. Fran had just received a scholarship to go to the CUA Law School.

It now looked as though a treasured friendship was about to be tested by the vast distance between San Francisco and the nation's capital.

While we continued to talk about these unfolding prospects, the sudden news of the assassination of Dr. Martin Luther King Jr., on April 4, 1968, struck the nation like a lightning bolt.

Classes were cancelled. University students in the metro area united to plan a service at Washington's Lafayette Park, across the street from the White House, to pray for national unity and peace.

Fran and I, along with Fran's classmate Marian Prio, whose father was an exiled former president of Cuba, rode together the several-mile distance to the White House while smoke and vandalism broke out in the streets of downtown Washington.

"Wow, there are so many fires," Marian observed from the back seat of my Pontiac as traffic bogged down to a full stop near Seventh Street, a corridor in which bands of angry youth were marauding in and out of looted stores.

Sirens blared everywhere. It quickly dawned on all three of us that the turmoil multiplying around us was just the beginning of something wildly out of control. We were smack in the middle of a full-scale urban riot.

"I don't think we are going anywhere," I said as Fran turned on the car radio and the news confirmed our worst suspicions.

"Oh, this is nothing," remarked Marian in her calm Latina voice meant to soothe our growing panic as the conflagration closed in. "When we lived in Havana in the early '50s," she continued, "we would sometimes have to duck on our school bus floor to dodge the shooting." She surveyed the thick smoke now approaching our car from nearby burning stores.

I saw an opening in the opposite lane of traffic heading out of the city, so I spun the wheel and hit the accelerator. Within seconds we were on our way out of the inner city and heading for Catholic University.

We passed a convoy of National Guard trucks speeding along in the opposite lane, coming down Michigan Avenue. Then we saw armed troops packed in the back of the trucks while heavy armaments followed. That afternoon, more than fifteen thousand soldiers entered the city to help police restore order.

The nation's capital would burn for days. Historic neighborhoods like Shaw, Columbia Heights, and areas of Fourteenth Street—centers of African American life—were almost completely destroyed. A dozen people lost their lives, and more than six thousand others were arrested. The riots devastated Washington's economy. Decades would pass before the city would fully recover.

It was a scene that we could never have imagined, and it was replicated in more than one hundred cities across the United States. The nation had entered a new era of racial tension. Peacemakers such as Bobby Kennedy and James Farmer were urging calm. They spoke of nonviolent social change in keeping with Dr. King's legacy. Other voices—on both the right and left—stoked embers of discord.

Within two months, Senator Robert Kennedy himself would be dead from an assassin's bullet. He was killed during that late spring's presidential campaign. For so many young people of our generation, hope and the idealism that fueled so much of the decade seemed to be giving way to a more cynical divide.

The conflict in Vietnam continued to escalate. It reached a peak that same year with the so-called Tet Offensive, a concerted effort by the North Vietnamese Army to overwhelm the government of South Vietnam. American causalities numbered in the tens of thousands, and the relentless heavy bombing of North Vietnam by the United States was doing little other than killing innocent civilians.

Amid the social turmoil and uncertainty that faced America, daily decisions still had to be made and life still required a game plan. My friendship with Fran had blossomed into full-blown love. I knew that living without her would be unthinkable. I could not contemplate the distance that would separate us as we completed our respective graduate degrees on opposite sides of the country. Nor could I afford to risk lifelong regret if I did not seize the moment to open my heart to her about what she meant to me.

During the summer break from the university, I invited Fran to Florida to meet my family. The boldness of such an invitation was not a complete surprise to Fran, but she was stunned when, during her stay, I proposed to her.

I asked her to marry me and move with me to California. I had so little to offer her except my love and a dream to become a college teacher of theology. I barely had enough money to afford an engagement ring. But Fran's feelings prevailed over her previous plans for law school. I was jubilant when she said yes with a beaming smile. She added that she'd apply for USF's graduate school as well.

The fall sped by, and I completed my studies at CUA. Fran and I married in Rhode Island during the snowy Christmas holidays, honeymooned in Montreal in the middle of blizzards, and were soon driving across the country to San Francisco. A new adventure was beginning.

Thanks to the parents of friends who lived in the City by the Bay, we found an apartment near the University of San Francisco and also found part-time jobs—Fran as a federal worker for VISTA in the San Francisco Regional Office, and I as a "detective" for Pinkerton Security, policing cable car conductors on the municipal railway. The job paid a little more per hour than the warehouse guard position I had sought originally.

California was very different from our East Coast environment. On weekends we took advantage of the outdoors as much as we could, traveling to the mountains near Lake Tahoe, exploring the spectacular coastline of Big Sur, and often picnicking in the wine country of northern California.

San Francisco was the center of the hippie culture of the late 1960s, which had been influenced by the beatnik culture of the 1950s, born in the very same city. The Golden Gate city seemed to have a long history of rebelling against the status quo.

A post–World War II generation questioned the rampant materialism of the nation's economic boom in those years. Artists, poets, and intellectuals considered the making of money destructive to the human spirit; their art, work, and discussions opened the way for the more socially conscious generation of the 1960s.

Our neighborhood in San Francisco was next to the University of San Francisco and only blocks from the Haight-Ashbury section of the city, ground zero for communal living, psychedelic music, and wafts of marijuana.

Two blocks south of our apartment on Golden Gate Avenue, members of the rock band Jefferson Airplane lived in a large white-columned house on Fulton Street. Not infrequently, the group would stage an impromptu free concert in nearby Golden Gate Park.

Fran and I loved sitting on the park grass under sunny clear skies watching all the bearded characters, including hippies and motorcycle gangs, nod their heads to the electric rhythms from the Airplane's flatbed truck.

USF was a good university but not nearly as strong academically in those days as CUA had been. USF made up for its thin course offerings in graduate theology by the warmth of its welcome and the novelty of an ecumenical faculty—a rarity then for Catholic theological schools.

The presence of fewer clergy, along with the less tradition-bound ways of California, provided the liberation I was hoping for in this new chapter of my life.

The year moved along as Fran and I settled into routines of

class, work, and weekend outings with new student friends, Bill and Carole Cotter, transplanted Rhode Islanders. Fran and Bill knew each other from their high school days, and Bill attended law school in San Francisco.

The culture of northern California with its breathtaking natural beauty, the high concentration of wealth, progressive politics, and the flavoring of eccentric characters was like nothing either of us had experienced.

One Saturday, our next-door neighbors, Noel and Nancy, a California couple about our age, invited us to their apartment to watch them feed their pet boa constrictor. We hadn't realized what this meant. The stomach-turning sight of the wiggling feet of a little white mouse being swallowed by a massive snake and the unsettling grins on our neighbor's faces confirmed our feelings that living in San Francisco could be hazardous to our mental state over the long run.

The newness and diversity of California were always head-turning and entertaining for us, but we missed our families back east. Besides that, our spirits ached to experience again the seasonal changes that marked the passage of time: spring's lush bursting forth and autumn's chill and colors.

By Christmas, my application to CUA for doctoral studies had been approved, and I had been awarded a graduate fellowship. I passed my comprehensive exams, and completed the requirements for the master's degree at USF. Fran and I headed back east.

We loaded our Volkswagen camper and once again drove across the country, thankful for the experience of California but excited by prospects of living closer to our families and friends.

Once back, we hit the ground running; I as a doctoral student, and Fran as a legislative aide to the U.S. Democratic senator from California, Alan Cranston.

Soon we had enough savings to scrape together a down payment for an old Victorian townhouse on Capitol Hill. After the proper amount of sweat equity and new paint, our home seemed to shine in the otherwise scruffy neighborhood, two blocks from congressional office buildings.

My doctoral dissertation was coming along. I had chosen to write about John Henry Newman, a nineteenth-century convert from Anglicanism to Catholicism, and later, a cardinal in the church, as well as a prolific writer. Newman's sanctity would be recognized in his canonization in 2019.

Newman drew my interest because of his thought on the role of the laity in the Catholic Church. His life, like mine, was marked by a series of separate chapters. Newman's openness to change and to finding the divinely designated path of one's life inspired and fascinated me.

His roots were in evangelical Protestantism. Ideology had no place in his life. Nor was he dominated by established patterns and the status quo; he was a perfect hero for a restless younger person setting out on life's excursion.

Newman's gifts as a writer and preacher touched me powerfully. He confirmed in me an earlier decision to stay with theology regardless of its potential to put food on the table.

In Newman's writings I found an explanation about how a person searched for the divine. For Newman, the human heart functions as God's built-in navigation system. Newman's own journey from evangelicalism to high church Anglicanism, then later Catholicism, was an exercise in discerning where the divine required a step forward. This process had collateral effects that could include loneliness, loss of friendships, and even ridicule. But over time, Newman found that listening to the signals of one's heart brought inner peace.

Newman's powerful poetic and lyrical writings, even in their aristocratic Victorian style, seemed like God's message affirming my decision to study theology as a layman.

As I looked on my newly minted doctorate in systematic theology in the spring of 1972, many wonderful surprises awaited.

Our first child, Ellen, arrived. Meghan and John would follow soon after.

Parenthood for both of us brought waves of joy and the sobering challenges of paying a mortgage. While searching for a teaching job, I went to work at the nearby U.S. House of Representatives for a joint committee of Congress. I was a staff researcher and helped plan hearings on such abstruse subjects as changing the federal government's fiscal year. It was far afield from the world of systematic theology, but it educated me on the structure of government and helped me pay our growing family's monthly bills, while the use of my new doctorate in theology awaited.

Then a Senate work colleague of Fran's told her about a job announcement for a Capitol Hill liaison for Catholic hospitals that she thought might interest me. It was a position at the United States Catholic Conference (USCC). The job description implied that advanced background in Catholicism might help a candidate's chances.

In the early 1970s, Catholic hospitals, still staffed and led by their founding religious orders, were the beneficiaries of millions of dollars in new federal money through the Medicare and Medicaid programs enacted during Lyndon Johnson's Great Society. As government involvement in health care grew, Catholic hospitals worked together to establish a lobbying presence in Congress. The position at the USCC functioned in that way.

My work experience in Congress, coupled with my doctorate in theology, gave me an edge over other applicants. I was offered the job.

On the staff of the USCC I would look out for the interests of some six hundred Catholic hospitals. It was not the college teacher post I had anticipated, but with the wisdom of Cardinal Newman, I took the development as just the kind of surprise that would lead to places where my abilities could be put to better use.

5

Call to Action

The United States Catholic Conference (USCC) was the national meeting place for the bishops of the United States. Its origins dated back to World War I, when it was a coordinating agency for Catholic chaplains serving in the armed forces. After the war, it provided a base to influence new national policies from a Catholic perspective in the postwar reconstruction period.

By the Second Vatican Council, the Catholic Conference was regarded as a template by the council for episcopal cooperation, in each country of the world.

I looked up at the massive statue of *Christ, the Light of the World*, designed by Notre Dame art professor Eugene Kommendi, overlooking the USCC's art deco entrance on Massachusetts Avenue. I paused and smiled with anticipation and irony as I entered the building marked by the initials of its previous nomenclature, NCWC (National Catholic Welfare Conference). *So this is where all that news of my youth was sourced*, I thought, as I opened the glass front door.

The job I began that morning would entail working with a Catholic sister in her role as interlocutor between Catholic hospitals and the federal government. Uncle Sam was channeling billions of new dollars to the nation's health providers. There was yet little by way of monitoring or controlling how these public monies were spent. Most delivery of health services at this time came through the nonprofit sector. The federal government was beginning to launch the tidal wave of regulation meant to bring order and quality to what the public was buying. It made sense for the Catholic sector, representing almost a fifth of the nation's hospital capacity, to have a seat at the table of Washington's discussions on health care.

These initial days at the USCC were exhilarating. I was no longer doing esoteric staff work for Congress and was now employed by a church-related institution. I was also learning about national health policy and the brilliant history of the Catholic sisters who had established networks of caring institutions in America, some dating back to the early eighteenth century.

This experience would also influence a later moment in my life when advocacy for the rights of elderly retired sisters became a cause for me. In the first days of my new USCC duties, however, I was gaining needed perspective on the vast institutional presence of the church.

I was interfacing with sisters and their hospitals, as well as with health policy wonks, unions, and community leaders. I digested volumes of background papers on the uneven accessibility of health care throughout the country, and spent hours at congressional oversight hearings on Capitol Hill.

For someone who had been riveted to a classroom desk for decades, this new exposure to the church's service was electrifying. I was getting to know the U.S. bishops and learning more about how the church was managed in each diocese. I watched the interactions of bishops for the first time and heard them talk about their experiences at the recently concluded Second Vatican Council.

Some members of the USCC staff had been legends to me during my seminary years. Msgr. George Higgins, who represented the long tradition of clergy chaplains in the union movement, was still an active force at the conference. Msgr. Higgins's extensive involvement on behalf of the newly formed United Farm Workers (UFW), comprising agricultural workers in California, was an example. Higgins had the entire hierarchy participating in a nationwide grape boycott to force growers to sit down and bargain with the UFW over wages and working conditions.

But the USCC was far more than a social justice lobby or a

meeting place for bishops. It was also a conglomeration of older organizations formed in the Catholic subculture of decades past, such as the National Conference of Catholic Women (NCCW) and the Catholic Youth Organization (CYO).

A variety of smaller entities representing nearly every dimension of Catholic life, from chaplains and deacons to Catholic schools, were housed at the USCC. The Office for Health and Hospitals, my domain, was just one of these groups.

Sister of Providence Virginia Schwager, a former hospital administrator, was the director of the Health and Hospitals office. She oversaw my work and connected me to the world of Catholic health care.

Agencies such as hospitals and nursing homes were largely founded by sisters—many from Europe—and were semi-independent from the day-to-day oversight of the American bishops. Nuns were expected to manage their own properties, raise funds for their ministries without the hierarchy's help, and stay clear of ethical conflicts in the practice of medical care.

Most bishops were standoffish and generally avoided the sisters' health-care ministry. Women religious liked it that way. They kept their distance from diocesan bureaucracies. Yet, because of this lack of contact, bishops often failed to appreciate Catholic health care's social influence and community impact.

It was no surprise that women religious in the health-care ministry were ambivalent about supporting an office for health care at the USCC. Sr. Virginia spent a great deal of her time assuring her sisters in Catholic health ministry that my office provided a valuable way to broaden interest and support for Catholic hospitals among church leaders while it represented the sisters' concerns on Capitol Hill.

While Sr. Virginia worked to smooth relations between religious and the nation's bishops, my duties involved participating in congressional hearings on health care and working with unions and nonprofit organizations in Washington that were advancing the case for national health insurance.

Walter Reuther, president of the United Auto Workers, had established the Committee for National Health Insurance (CNHI) in 1970. Thanks to Msgr. George Higgins, the USCC was a founding committee member, along with other faith-related and community-based organizations and unions.

Congresswoman Martha Griffiths of Michigan and Senator Ted Kennedy of Massachusetts had cosponsored legislation to bring about national health insurance, and the CNHI worked to build broad bipartisan support for the measure.

The weekly legislative briefings of the CNHI provided one of the best classes for me in health policy, enabling me to understand the social benefits that could be achieved through broad health coverage of the citizenry.

Years later, this early exposure to CNHI helped me to appreciate the history behind the indispensable role that Catholic sisters would play in the successful enactment in 2010 of the Affordable Care Act during the Obama administration.

After mere weeks on the job, I was sent to Sedalia, Colorado, to a meeting of diocesan leaders—bishops as well as their Catholic Charities directors—to brief them on national health reform.

This was my first speaking engagement. I worked hard to engage the audience.

The spirit of the faculty at St. John's inspired me as I made the case for fairness and justice in health-care access and helped the audience to see that health coverage was a corollary of papal and conciliar social teaching.

My high-spirited enthusiasm for my new job and the exposure it provided me to the church's social justice networks influenced my growing resolve to stay with this more activist career path. My thoughts of teaching college students began to fade.

Not everything at the USCC was perfect. The chief of its governmental affairs was a retired newspaper reporter, Jim Robinson, who spent much of his time policing young USCC staffers like me so that we did not get in the way of the conference's congressional lobbying priorities: fighting abortion and obtaining federal tax credits for Catholic schools.

According to Robinson, national health insurance and issues of poverty and civil rights took second seat to institutional protections. He did not want anyone at the USCC muddying the waters in political coalition work with other groups or in what he called "pie-in-the-sky" social dreams.

Robinson had influential allies within the legal staff, the USCC press office, and the pro-life staff, and he thrived on combat with those on the USCC social advocacy team, including this young neophyte representing Catholic health care.

Skirmishes with the USCC's principal lobbyist were weekly affairs. I learned to cope with the grumbling and to maneuver around him on more than one occasion. But Robinson's stance was more reflective of the conservative bishops than the labor union progressives with whom I also worked and whose coalition campaigned for broader health-care coverage.

Not infrequently, after having to defer to the chief USCC lobbyist, I would commute home stewing about the fact that the work for social justice on Capitol Hill seemed of secondary importance to the bishops. I promised myself that someday I would talk with the bishop running the USCC about this. At this stage, I was too new and far too low on the totem pole to have that access.

Then the annual employee picnic took place on a spring afternoon at Fort Hunt Park in nearby Virginia. It provided an informal occasion to meet the twenty or so priests who held most of the top jobs at USCC. Almost all of them resided in a small apartment building in northeast Washington near the Franciscan monastery. The staff house of the USCC was a kind of clergy clubhouse. There was a good deal of drinking there as well as church chinwag out of earshot of the rest of us employees who were laypeople. The USCC annual picnic, however, enabled all of us—priest and lay—to interact in a relaxed atmosphere. We were encouraged to bring our families.

This particular sunny and hot day, smoke from the barbeques filled the grounds as children played tag, grownups tossed baseballs, and battling street music genres from our maintenance staff competed from boom boxes. Lush trees surrounded the grassy island of colorful blankets, while small groupings of people laughed and sipped beer from plastic cups.

Fran and I entered a park shelter where we joined a line for hot dogs and potato salad. A couple of priests dressed in white short-sleeved shirts and black pants were walking down the line in the opposite direction, shaking hands and introducing themselves. When they reached us, I realized that one of the priests was the man in charge of running the entire conference: General Secretary James Rausch, a newly ordained bishop from Minnesota.

I introduced Fran and answered the bishop's friendly questions about my recent arrival at the USCC. When I informed Bishop Rausch that I had just graduated from CUA the previous spring with a doctorate in theology, he seemed mildly surprised. He then congratulated us on our infant daughter, who was fast asleep in Fran's shoulder sling, and went on to shake the hand of the next person behind us.

This chance encounter with Bishop Rausch resulted in a call a few days later. The general secretary wanted to hear more about my theological studies.

When I entered Rausch's smoke-filled office, he asked me to take a seat and began a conversation about the bishops' plans for the observance of the nation's two hundredth anniversary.

"I'd like you to think about taking on the job of coordinating that effort."

I knew little about the church's bicentennial program at that point, but I was aware that its focus was on social justice, and it was led by one of the most respected voices in the hierarchy, the archbishop of Detroit. I tried to suppress a smile and acted as though this unexpected and thrilling news was perfectly normal. I did not want Rausch to change his mind about offering this job to this twenty-eight-year-old neophyte.

"We are planning to devote the year of 1976 to a conversation on justice in America," Bishop Rausch continued. "Cardinal John Dearden has agreed to chair the program." Dearden was deeply revered by many and a legend at Vatican II.

"We are likening the project to what the Latin American bishops did in Medellín, Colombia, five years ago," said Rausch, who was known to talk about his initiatives the same way that Hollywood studios talk about a potential film with investors.

I was vaguely familiar with Medellín and the now-emergent

liberation theology of Latin America that got kick-started there. The 1968 meeting was considered a watershed event in church history. During Medellín, the hierarchy of the South had taken a major step away from a historical alignment with the elite aristocracy and ruling power in Latin America. The bishops there adopted a totally new pastoral approach requiring the church to identify more explicitly with the poor and with indigenous cultures. Pastors, bishops, and priests would empower such populations to exercise their human dignity and demand more justice and equality.

As Bishop Rausch continued to share the plans of the American bishops, I began to feel woefully inexperienced. But somehow, I also felt that I could not let this great opportunity pass.

The Nixon administration had already announced its plans for the nation's observance of the bicentennial. The plan was anything but revolutionary. John Warner, a former secretary of the navy and then husband of banking heiress Catherine Mellon, was coordinating Nixon's plans, which amounted to Main Street parades and nationalistic celebrations to counteract the antiwar and civil protests dominating the country's headlines.

This was the age of the "silent majority." The nation's anniversary coming in the middle of widening social unrest was a perfect occasion to manifest the underreported happiness, tranquility, and pride that American's felt on this national birthday.

Bishop Rausch was telling me that the Catholic bishops in the United States saw the years leading up to 1976 differently. The Vietnam War, where thousands of people had lost their lives, was coming to an end. The House Judiciary Committee was investigating the Watergate break-in and possible breaches of trust by the White House. Violent crime rates and unemployment in the cities were at a historic high.

It was not a time for parades, the bishops thought.

Catholic leaders appeared to represent the only major national organization willing to embark on a serious conversation about American ideals and the attainability of justice and fairness for large segments of the U.S. population.

"I'll do it," I blurted out before Rausch went further.

Within weeks of the offer, I had left the Catholic hospital lobby job and assumed my new post as executive director of the National Conference of Catholic Bishops' (NCCB) ad hoc Committee for the Catholic Observance of the Bicentennial.

I had never met a cardinal before, and now I was working for one of the finest of them, John Dearden. He played a major role in the formation of the decree on the laity of the Second Vatican Council. Rhode Island born and Cleveland raised, Dearden had been a tradition-bound conservative known by the nickname "Iron John" until a conversion experience at the Second Vatican Council changed his view. His previously self-assured style of leading gave way to a genuinely new and intense effort to see God working through the lives of everyone.

Returning from the council, Dearden was elected as the first president of the U.S. bishops' conference. Immediately, he launched a series of new consultative configurations both in his Detroit archdiocese and within the national meeting place of bishops to encourage more lay participation in church decision-making.

Seven years after the founding of what was known as the NCCB and the USCC, Cardinal Dearden, the NCCB/USCC's founding president, was suggesting the creation of an additional project to capture lay interest and input in the church's agenda in the United States.

He proposed a major examination of justice, in stages, to include local planning and consultative meetings, leading up to a national congress in the fall of 1976. The aim was to propose steps to promote social justice at all levels of the church in this country.

It was an ambitious undertaking. Now, almost by the accident of attending the company picnic, I had been selected to help direct this exciting program.

"He's not the best we could probably find, but he'll do for now," said Cardinal John Krol of Philadelphia, president of the NCCB, when he introduced me to the governing committee of some sixty bishops who supervised the entire conference.

Krol had invited me to stand up from my chair at the back of the meeting room, and he continued to wise-crack about the bicentennial project, which he considered to be untimely, in view of the International Eucharistic Congress planned for the very same year in Philadelphia, the "City of Brotherly Love." Krol's sarcasm was more than just playful. Though a friend of Cardinal Dearden, Cardinal Krol represented an opposite polarity in the U.S. hierarchy, one more comfortable with a traditional approach to clergy-laity relations and cool to the church reforms called for by Vatican II. Those in his camp were the foot draggers when it came to anything that might lessen their sovereign role in church affairs. They were obsessed with protecting local diocesan autonomy and did not want this new Vatican II invention, a bishop's conference, infringing on their role.

Within months of my accepting this new position, Archbishop Joseph L. Bernardin, another key bishop chosen to help lead Cardinal Dearden's Bicentennial Committee, called together a planning subcommittee to discuss a plan of action and adopt a theme for the 1976 conference on justice. (Bernardin would later leave the committee in 1975 to take on a new role as president of the NCCB.) Michael Novak—a scholar at the American Enterprise Institute, a pro-business lobby, and a member of Bernardin's committee—played a creative role in conceptualizing the bishops' plans for the bicentennial, including suggesting the theme of *Liberty and Justice for All*. Novak thought this theme could be explored within the context of the concentric circles in which most Americans live: personhood, family, neighborhood, nationhood, ethnicity and race, work, church, and the broader global community—humankind.

Ironically, it was Novak's lifelong friendship with sociologist and *Chicago Daily News* columnist Fr. Andrew Greeley that would lead to a series of unrelenting public attacks on the bishops' bicentennial plan by the Chicago priest.

Novak had asked the chairman of the planning group, Archbishop Bernardin, to appoint Greeley to the group's membership. Because of Greeley's prickly disposition, Bernardin said no to Novak's request. Three years prior, in 1972, the U.S. bishops had commissioned Greeley to write a profile of the American priesthood based on two years of research. Greeley reported that dissatisfaction with church leadership among the priests was widespread. The hierarchy refused to publish the results. Fr. Greeley then went public and called the bishops morally, intellectually, and religiously bankrupt.

Now Fr. Greeley learned from Novak that he was considered unsuitable for Bernardin's subcommittee. The combative clergyman was furious, and possibly influenced his subsequent public criticisms of the bishops' program.

The bishops' plan for the bicentennial progressed nonetheless. The NCCB launched its first listening conference in the winter of 1975. The idea was to invite a wide sector of people to talk to the bishops about justice in the church and society and to blend what was heard at these hearings with parish-based recommendations nationwide. This input would shape the agenda for a major meeting on justice in the fall of the nation's two hundredth birthday.

This novel series of hearings was an idea suggested over the home dinner table by my wife, Fran, whose work in the U.S. Senate provided extensive experience in planning such sessions. I passed the suggestion on to Cardinal Dearden, who immediately saw its potential both in pastoral and cultural terms. He thought it was an especially American way of proceeding.

Dearden's committee kicked off the first hearing on a snowy day in February in the auditorium of Washington's Theological College at Catholic University—the very seminary I had once attended.

The cardinal opened the hearing with the promise to undertake the widest possible sharing of assessments of how the American Catholic community might contribute to the quest for liberty and justice. A dozen bishops and the local cardinal, William Baum, joined the hearing committee, along with lay members of the Bicentennial Committee. Those testifying included local community leaders as well as notables in Catholic life such as University of Notre Dame president Theodore Hesburgh, CSC; theologian and future cardinal Avery Dulles, SJ; and Xavier University alum Alexis Herman, a diocesan Catholic Charities director and future cabinet member in the Clinton administration. Lines of everyday Catholics surprised us with their interest as witnesses and audience in the new listening program.

The quality of the discussion kept things moving over the

course of two days. The positive atmosphere and the lively back and forth between witnesses and panel gave those present the impression that they were taking part in an exciting new way for the church to engage its members.

Just weeks following the opening program, however, Fr. Andrew Greeley launched a public broadside. He filled an entire insert in the *National Catholic Reporter* newspaper, taking on the NCCB observance as the creation of a "new" social action movement, which he called amateurish. He battered the NCCB's published parish materials to promote local conversations as unscholarly and hypocritical. "When the National Conference of Catholic Bishops confronts me about liberty and justice," Greeley seethed, "I feel like laughing in their faces."

The NCCB program had barely taken off when this celebrity figure and columnist introduced a narrative about the bicentennial program that, though vengeful and unfair, would be hard to shake.

Compounding the committee's public relations problem was the reality that almost no money had been raised by the NCCB to conduct its bicentennial activities. With only three staff members, little could be done to correct the image of the program that Greeley presented: a rebellion of leftists.

Fr. Greeley's writings were armchair fiction for the most part; we had no budget, and our only activity at this point was holding the hearings every other month. But Greeley seemed to be enjoying himself in this payback to the NCCB, which had both rejected his research on the priesthood and his involvement in the bicentennial plans. What no one, not even Greeley, anticipated was the way his polemic would be adopted by those on the right, who also helped to amplify the project in the public's mind as some form of grand conspiracy.

As the bishops moved on to San Antonio in April 1975 to continue the bicentennial listening sessions, they made more room for the voices from neighborhoods and parishes, especially on the issue of immigration. The slightly more local flavor began to demonstrate the potential these forums had for candid conversations between the hierarchy and the faithful who saw the church as an agent for justice.

Worker priest George Higgins joined the bishops on their hearing panel and expressed his admiration for the strength of witness testimony on workers' rights and the flaws in U.S. immigration policy. Higgins used the occasion to scold Fr. Greeley, a good friend, for his prejudicial criticisms of the bicentennial program, calling his writing "overkill, shrill, and unprofessional."

By June, Dearden's committee landed in St. Paul, Minnesota, where owners of small family farms lined up to be heard along with Native Americans, who talked about their difficult history with the American government and with Christian missionaries.

By discernible degrees, bicentennial participants began to shift the focus on justice in American society to policies and practices within Catholicism. Testimony by farmers on national agricultural policies that were contributing to the decline in family farming morphed into questions about the church's unfair decisions to assign priests to rural parishes as either training grounds or retirement homes. An exchange between the bishops and participants on the defense of the unborn evolved into a discussion of the church's overall lack of advocacy for the progress of women. The discriminatory practices of U.S. society that locked out masses of people from equal opportunity morphed into a review of the church's exclusion and harsh treatment of divorced couples, former priests, and gay members of the Catholic faithful.

The Call to Action hearing panel in Newark, New Jersey. Right to left: Bishop John Mugovero of Brooklyn; labor priest Msgr. George Higgins; Frank Butler, staff director for the NCCB Program on Justice; Cardinal John Dearden of Detroit; Archbishop Peter Gerety of Newark; and Bishop James Rausch, NCCB general secretary. (Credit: D. J. Zehnder, Montclair, New Jersey)

Labor leader and civil rights activist Cesar Chavez addresses Cardinal Dearden's Call to Action hearings in Sacramento in October 1975 (Credit: Willig)

By August 1975, these meetings had caught the attention of the *New York Times*. The newspaper sent a reporter to the bicentennial listening session in Georgia. The *Times'* religion editor, Kenneth Briggs, found himself sitting under a spacious green revival tent in Tidy Creek, Georgia, just north of Atlanta, with nearly four hundred people crowding in where the bishops gathered at a dusty mountain campsite. In that space, a dozen bishops took testimony from a mixed assembly of the rural poor. Cane harvesters, mill workers, migrant farm laborers, and coal miners discussed the economic pressures on the American family, their difficulties keeping food on the table, and occupational health hazards.

Briggs's articles in the *Times* drew national attention and were unreservedly praising of a program so out of the ordinary. "No endeavor" dealing with the nation's bicentennial observance, said Briggs, "has required more time and energy than the Catholic concept."

Such judgments were instrumental in our experiencing a huge uptick of new voices wishing to be heard, including luminaries such as Dorothy Day, cofounder of the Catholic Worker movement, and UFW founder Cesar Chavez. Hearings included other well-known Americans like Senator Walter Mondale; Bayard Rustin, a brilliant tactician for the passage of the Civil Rights Act and chief architect of the 1963 March on Washington; and Chilean human rights activist and a victim of torture, Dr. Sheila Cassidy.

Catholic Worker activist Dorothy Day talks with Frank Butler prior to Cardinal Dearden's Call to Action hearings in Newark, New Jersey, December 1975

Public interest in the NCCB's program continued to increase as the bicentennial year opened and national official observances took on a less serious and more traditionally celebratory cast with parades and fireworks.

Yet, just as the pace of work seemed beyond the capacity of our three-person staff, Bishop Rausch added more responsibilities to my daily duties. He appointed me to direct the domestic policy staff of the USCC.

The USCC had an ancient history in Washington, influencing social legislation at the federal level, including the Social Security Act. The Domestic Policy Office was a successor to this tradition, comprising policy wonks who prepared congressional testimony, interacted with nonprofit organizations, and kept the U.S. bishops informed on national developments impacting the common good. Supervision of this office was now my added duty.

General Secretary Rausch had become convinced that the outcomes of the bicentennial hearings were likely to influence the priorities of the USCC for years to come. In his mind, linking the

NCCB's program with the domestic policy staff now made sense. But for me it meant more work-related stress.

As a thirty-year-old with a growing family—now two young daughters—and a two-hour commute each working day, I saw the new assignment, while a wonderful opportunity, as not exactly welcome news. In addition, several of the posts in the Domestic Policy Office were empty at the time, and I would have to find candidates to fill them.

The hearings for the NCCB were now completed. Local parish-based discussions throughout the country had produced a boxcar load of written reports and recommendations that continued to pile up as planning got under way for the National Bicentennial Conference to be held in Detroit, Michigan.

A conference theme was inspired by Pope Paul's 1971 statement on the eightieth anniversary of the first social encyclical, *Rerum Novarum*. Pope Paul's message was known as the *Call to Action* (*CTA*) because he invited the entire church not only to study Catholic social principles but, more importantly, to take actions guided by those principles. The pope stated,

> It is to all Christians that we address a fresh and insistent call to action. It is not enough to recall principles . . . and utter prophetic denunciations; these words will lack real weight unless they are accompanied by effective action. (*CTA* 48)

The Detroit gathering was all about working up a plan of action for justice in the Catholic Church of the United States. This would be based on the mountains of input from Catholic parishes and the seven national hearings.

Our three-person bicentennial staff began to grow. Sr. Maria Riley, OP, from the Adrian Michigan Dominican Sisters, dropped by my office one day when I was struggling through some planning for the Detroit meeting. It had been twenty years since I had last seen her, and I did not recognize this sister who inquired about volunteer opportunities for the bicentennial program. All I knew was that a Sr. Maria seated before me had three months of summer sabbatical time on her hands and wanted to help with our program.

Laughter exploded when the two of us suddenly and simultaneously realized that I had been Maria's fifth-grade student at Our Lady of Lourdes Catholic School in Melbourne, Florida, in the mid-1950s. Maria, known then as Sister Amabilis, had been one of my favorite teachers. Once again, I felt the touch of Providence in my good fortune.

Maria Riley later would become an international voice for human rights and the plight of women in poverty. But at this moment, I invited her to help immediately with the design process for what was now being called the "Call to Action Conference."

Sr. Maria was a whiz. She developed a fascinating process of decision-making based on religious community life that proved valuable in reaching consensus over controversial issues of our bicentennial program.

Next, I added Sr. Alice Gallin, OSU, a history professor from the College of New Rochelle, who had written to me to express a willingness to lend her talent to the planning. As a young woman during World War II, Alice had been a military intelligence analyst in the nation's capital. Her brainy and calm demeanor told me that she would be just the kind of person to bring order to the unanticipated quantity of parish and diocesan input.

Sr. Margaret Cafferty, PVBM, joined the team shortly thereafter. As a Catholic Charities worker, she brought a wonderful skill set. Margaret enlisted diocesan Catholic Charities' directors as the local organizers for the nine-member delegations that each diocese was asked to assemble for our gathering in Detroit. I had met Margaret at the University of Notre Dame's annual gathering of the Catholic Committee on Urban Ministry (CCUM), a loose federation of clergy and laity working for social change. With the help of the CCUM founder, Chicago's famed Msgr. Jack Egan, I was able to convince Margaret to leave her work as a community organizer on the Catholic Charities staff and play an important role in coordinating diocesan participants.

The CCUM network was filled with intellectual talent. David O'Brien, a Holy Cross professor, had a long affiliation with the

Catholic social justice movement. Sporting a flattop haircut, O'Brien looked more like a scrappy Marine than the gentle teacher of American church history that he was. He, too, agreed to an invitation to join the NCCB bicentennial staff, bringing a sharp analytic mind and lyrical writing gifts to bear on Cardinal Dearden's committee and the Call to Action communications.

As the year passed swiftly, the Domestic Policy Office also had a growing workload. Out of necessity, I begged for more staff help from the USCC's front office. I received a green light to hire two new policy analysts. I found John Carr, a Catholic Charities worker from Minneapolis, and Charlotte Mahoney, a social worker from New York, with expertise in the fields of aging and health care.

Along with John Carr and Charlotte Mahoney, we were able to add to our staff Msgr. Frank Lally, a Boston pastor and editor of the archdiocesan *Pilot* newspaper. The addition of this legendary ghost writer for Cardinal Richard Cushing was thanks to a fellow Bostonian, Fr. Bryan Hehir, director of the international side of our social justice office. Msgr. Lally became the leader of the entire conference's social justice department, offering depth, editorial experience, and keen social analysis that would move the USCC into the ranks of influential Washington think tanks and public policy advocates.

The visibility of the bicentennial program, combined with innumerable interactions within the frenetic world of social activism, had me quietly moaning from exhaustion as I commuted home each night. I did not want to disappoint those who gambled on my young leadership. When acid reflux became a frequent occurrence, I'd pop Rolaids and pray that it was only a stomach reaction—and chase away thoughts of an early demise.

As October 1976 approached, more than 1,350 voting delegates to the Detroit conference had been nominated by the nation's dioceses, and the finishing touches were being made to the preparatory documents—eight working papers on the original subjects chosen by Dearden's committee two years prior: personhood, family, neighborhood, nationhood, ethnicity and race, work, church, and humankind.

Nine-member diocesan delegations from 160 dioceses had taken part in sixteen preparatory training meetings that Sr. Margaret Cafferty conducted throughout the country over the course of weeks. Simultaneously, Margaret rehearsed with more than a hundred diocesan Catholic Charities' directors we deployed as Call to Action conference facilitators. Everyone had prepared, and all seemed ready.

When opening day arrived, registrations went smoothly as 110 bishops—a third of the U.S. hierarchy—and their diocesan delegations began to arrive at Detroit's famous Book Cadillac Hotel in downtown Detroit, only blocks from the cavernous Cobo Convention site where the Call to Action conference was to take place.

To our surprise, a small army of journalists showed up early. This was one aspect of the event for which we were not so well prepared. With little support from the USCC's communications staff, we did the best we could to manage an extemporaneous news conference.

From the beginning, the press showed its natural skepticism over anything that purported to represent a "listening" process in the Catholic Church. Bishops, it seemed, were mostly known for their endless streams of censures. Moreover, the Call to Action's reformist image was firmly fixed in the public's mind thanks to the relentless Fr. Greeley, whose columns predicted knee-jerk reactions and utter chaos. Catholic conservatives had been typecasting the program as a leftist insurrection.

It was not surprising, then, that the first news stories on the Detroit meeting described the event as disgruntled lay Catholics calling for radical change. These stories oversimplified a respectful listening process conducted through a thought-out process that had lasted more than two years. The news reports thus played down what was a consensus-building conference to strengthen the church's social justice work. Call to Action urged change, but its resolutions were worded with care. Where we did not reach consensus, there was often urging of further dialogue.

Media audiences are built on conflict, not accord. Reporters sharpened their narrative about the historic assembly. *Time* magazine led with opening story lines: "Women priests. Married priests. A more tolerant attitude toward birth control and homosexuality. Those were among the 182 proposals issued in Detroit. . . ."

While most of the nearly two hundred Call to Action resolutions called for intensified measures to combat racism, promote economic justice, and foster international peacebuilding, headlines characterized the event as an act of dissent.

Call to Action admittedly had drawbacks. Cardinal John Dearden himself later criticized its overly ambitious agenda and the haste to rush through some topics that deserved far more extensive debate. Nonetheless, Dearden found the two-year consultation culminating in the Detroit event both conscientious and sincere in its efforts to experiment with a new way for the people of God to work together on issues deserving Christian action.

In his letter in the days that followed, addressed to the then apostolic delegate to the United States, Archbishop Jean Jadot—who had accompanied Dearden to the Detroit conference—the cardinal said that participants "manifested a magnificent spirit of Christian community." Dearden stated that, Call to Action represented "a very positive and true step forward on the part of the Church in the United States."

That sentiment was not shared by the NCCB's new president at that time, Archbishop Bernardin. Bernardin, no longer a member of Cardinal Dearden's planning committee but deeply familiar with the Call to Action plan, quickly distanced the entire NCCB from the Detroit event, charging in a press release that the event was the product of special-interest groups. Archbishop Bernardin was fully aware of Pope Paul VI's reactions to news headlines in the *Herald American*, which the pope read daily. The newspaper cast the Call to Action meeting as an uprising.

Two years of goodwill, built up by patient listening and raising expectations about the laity and hierarchy working together to set a path for social action, were counteracted by Bernardin's precipitous public comments to reassure especially those in Rome that all was under control at the NCCB.

There was no time to absorb Bernardin's unexpected and quick maneuvering. He continued to issue bold dictums, appointing a task force to take over the Call to Action program, and shutting down Dearden's ad hoc NCCB Bicentennial Committee.

The new Bernardin task force was populated by cardinals who from the very beginning had shown no interest in Dearden's project. They included John Carberry, the cardinal archbishop of St. Louis; John Krol of Philadelphia; and William Baum, the cardinal archbishop of Washington.

The mission of the task force was to decide where to go from there.

As the weeks unfolded, and with the abrupt end of Cardinal Dearden's committee, I returned to my duties in the Domestic Policy Office, shocked and disheartened to see such an exercise of raw power. Bernardin's unilateral actions reflected the worst dynamics of church government, where decisions are made to impress and assure those at the top, but where the feelings and concerns of those at the bottom—in this case, thousands of parishioners—were summarily ignored. It was a managerial flaw that other bishops exhibited as well and would eventually be viewed as a causal factor in the scandalous cover-up and the injurious mishandling of clergy sexual abuse.

Within weeks, the new Bernardin task force was convened but had no clue of what to do. Archbishop Bernardin surprisingly passed staffing responsibilities on to me, and I was asked to be present for the task force meetings.

The group's review of the Detroit's conference recommendations found little that was actually troublesome in its resolutions. Stronger efforts to combat racism, build a culture of peace and justice in the marketplace, enhance protections for the unborn, and create a more robust ministry for marriage and the family were examples of the nearly two hundred resolutions that the new committee surveyed. These goals were mostly affirmations of the pastoral and social direction already under way in the Catholic Church.

"This whole thing has been a complete disaster," Cardinal Krol barked, with the other cardinals looking on. The Philadelphia cardinal had opposed Dearden's plan from the start. He declined to participate in any of the bicentennial hearings or to conduct any archdiocesan parish consultations. His resources and attention had been solely concentrated on the Forty-First International Eucharistic Conference in Philadelphia, held the previous August.

"No matter what these people may have been told," griped Bishop Joseph McNicholas, an auxiliary bishop of St. Louis designated by the elderly Cardinal Carberry to represent him on the task force, "we don't run the church by consensus."

Remarkably, most of the task force's meeting time did not center on the Call to Action conference at all. A papal document published in Latin called *Inter Insignores*, not then available to the English-speaking world, was of curious if not obsessive interest to Bernardin's task force. Through it, the Vatican had closed the door firmly on the possibility of ordaining women to the priesthood.

Bernardin, who was present at the task force's meeting, was anxious to let the document speak for the entire U.S. hierarchy in response to the Call to Action resolution dealing with the ordination question.

Conferees in Detroit had asked for "a more fully developed position on the ordination of women to sacred orders." They wanted a study and results presented within a year. Study or not, Bernardin wanted the Vatican's new document to serve as the NCCB's response.

As for the rest of the Call to Action resolutions, Bernardin announced that he'd ask the NCCB's associate secretary, Dominican priest Thomas Kelly, to prepare a draft document that could be used as the basis of the response from the U.S. hierarchy. The full NCCB comprising the nation's Catholic bishops would meet in Chicago in five months.

The task of writing bishops' pastoral letters and public statements often fell on the shoulders of senior NCCB/USCC staff and was supervised by bishops' committees. In the case of the Call to Action program, the logical choice would have been the social development staff, where skilled writers such as Msgr. Frank Lally were ready and willing to rise to the moment and where staff involvement in the Call to Action process was both extensive and open-minded.

Yet Bernardin's choice of Kelly meant that more conservative points of view were needed. Kelly turned wordsmithing work over to the USCC communications director, Russell Shaw, the in-house skeptic of the bicentennial project. In Kelly's understanding of Bernardin's mind, it seemed, it was far more important to assure Rome that the Pandora's box of church reform and lay participation that the NCCB just opened would be closed tightly.

Over the next several months, several of Russell Shaw's drafts circulated within the NCCB. Partially coauthored by Cardinal William Baum, the drafts stressed the importance of the hierarchy itself, referring to the bishops sixteen times within the first five pages.

There was no reference to the people of God, as Vatican II described the church. The draft's reference to social justice was, as anticipated, weak and concessionary. "Consultation" the draft stated, ". . . cannot be a substitute for teaching ministry." Even for Bernardin's conservative task force, the draft was raising questions.

Bernardin, fearing a strongly negative reaction by his onetime mentor, Cardinal Dearden, then turned to Father Bryan Hehir, chief USCC international policy advisor, to get involved in the process. Hehir, a brilliant young priest, teaching once a week at Harvard while holding down the USCC's staff policy analyst job, was willing to help.

Hehir took strong exception to Bernardin's decision to allow a conservative journalist to shape the ecclesiology that would undergird such an important statement. Meanwhile, Cardinal Dearden refused to continue to stand on the sidelines. I had sent the cardinal a copy of Shaw's draft, and he concluded that an important good-faith effort of thousands of Catholics was not being given fair consideration. "Iron John," as Dearden had once been known, had had it with Bernardin's calculating management of the post–Call to Action conference period.

The cardinal wrote to Bernardin stating that he would publicly disclaim any association with Shaw's draft when the bishops gathered in Chicago. He made it abundantly clear that he viewed the document as vastly lacking in substance and tone, and completely out of sync with Vatican II.

Bernardin knew that Dearden was not bluffing. The NCCB could not afford the embarrassment of Cardinal Dearden's open rebellion. Bernardin had already upset Dearden with his impulsive moves as NCCB president to discredit the Call to Action conference and consultative process. Bernardin knew as well that Dearden was not without special influence and voice in Rome. Bernardin began to rethink his approach.

By early April 1977, the revised version of the conference's draft statement, now in its eighth edition, bore sparse resemblance to the conservative first versions. By then, the task of writing had been taken over by Bernardin himself and reflected significant concessions to Dearden. It was now more in line with conciliar theology.

Dearden communicated to Bernardin that he would not stand in the way of a bishops' debate on Bernardin's draft. But Dearden's acceptance would not matter. The drama had taken a toll on the Detroit cardinal. Bernardin's initial panic after the Call to Action and the frenzied efforts he took to shut out Dearden and distance the NCCB from his program proved too much on Dearden's system. He suffered a major heart attack the week before the bishops were to meet in Chicago.

Thankfully, Dearden survived, but he missed an important meeting that he longed to attend in which the nation's three hundred bishops gathered at the Palmer House Hotel in Chicago, where they considered the bicentennial program and their collective response.

Notwithstanding the absence of Cardinal Dearden, the bishops surprised everyone by praising the bicentennial program for its collaborative nature. The bishops underscored their support for the fundamental vision of *Lumen Gentium*, a horizontal architecture for the church that described Catholicism as the people of God. The U.S. bishops conceded that in any process of dialogue in the church, bishops need to listen, as all Christians do, for the voice of the Spirit in the church—a point that Cardinal Dearden had stressed repeatedly throughout the consultation.

Most significantly, the bishops did not endorse Bernardin's initial efforts to distance the NCCB from the Detroit recommendations, nor did they back his hurried judgment of the meeting as unrepresentative and extremist. They acknowledged that bishops had learned much about the needs of their people and about the problems of justice and peace in their communities, and they pledged themselves to a serious consideration of follow-up.

Within months, the bishops adopted a five-year programmatic framework titled "To Do the Work of Justice," which moved social justice to a prominent position in the church in the United States. It began with an agreement to issue joint pastoral letters on war and peace, the nation's economy, and on racism. A methodology of consultation and listening borrowed from the bicentennial process became the routine way of preparing such national reflections.

Nonetheless, opposition to the Detroit event continued in conservative circles. Right-wing pundits chastised the hierarchy for their tepid acquiescence to a liberal agenda of listening and progressive reform. Only a year after the bishops' pledges in Chicago to listen more, as Dearden's program had urged, Pope John Paul II began an era of church leadership favoring a trend back to traditional and hierarchical church governance.

The opposition notwithstanding, Call to Action and the bicentennial consultation continued to work its influence for positive change. As decades passed, it would be seen as an influential moment in Catholic life when social justice began to be more fully integrated into the church's institutional life and mission in the United States. Today, with the church at a crossroads following worldwide revelations about clergy sexual abuse and the clerical wall of separation and secrecy that enabled it, I wonder if Call to Action can offer an important lesson as the church continues to struggle to engage the whole People of God.

Despite longer-term positive effects, Call to Action never quite shook off its rabble-rousing image. Bernardin's impulsive actions to shut down the process just after the Detroit event in 1976 were remembered long after the more circumspect and positive declarations of the National Conference of Catholic Bishops.

As I commuted to and from work each long day in the immediate years following Call to Action, I often thought about both the good achieved and the stifling resistance to change and fear that dominates Catholic life. These reflections triggered memories of my formative years at St. John's Seminary, when young faculty injected our classrooms with newer scholarship and social awareness that upset the comfortable certainty of Catholicism in a previous era. These young priests were eager to respond to what Vatican II asked of all Catholics in calling them to a more engaged relationship with the world, yet these priests still paid a great price for their ideas and actions. The local bishop who oversaw their work was quicker to discipline them than to listen to what they were saying.

Call to Action also presented a moment of opportunity for the U.S. hierarchy to respond to the Second Vatican Council. Call to Action was undertaken as a moment of dialogue on society and the church in matters of liberty and justice. The program had provided an imperfect but sincere attempt for members of the church to be heard and to listen to one another as they sought together to map out directions for the future. Despite this noble aspiration, for some in the hierarchy, Call to Action was a threat to the established order, especially as its process exposed injustices within the life of the church itself that required discussion and resolution.

In the end, while the hierarchy seemed supportive of stronger stances on social justice, it was lightning fast in closing off dialogue on matters some thought to be injustices in Catholic life: the exclusion of women from the priesthood, the treatment of divorced people, the rights of parents to regulate birth, the way gay people are treated, and inflexibility on a married clergy. These important issues remain unresolved to this day.

I found myself growing disheartened over the course of events following the Call to Action and began to look for other ways of contributing to the life of the Catholic community. I still wanted more than ever to help my beloved church, whose rank-and-file members I had heard during the bicentennial hearings. Still, I longed for a more generous, less fearful environment in which to labor than I had found at the NCCB, where institutional protection and preserving the status quo impeded forward movement.

I was deeply grateful for my seven years at the conference of bishops, most especially so because of the collaboration with Cardinal Dearden, an inspiring hero whose experience at Vatican II gave him an unshakable conviction that the Spirit works in each of us. This wisdom would serve me well as I grew in my responsibilities and leadership later in life.

Even the disappointing careerist decisions of Cardinal Bernardin, designed to distance the NCCB from Call to Action and curry favor in Rome, contained valuable life lessons. Years later, after the cardinal had contracted terminal cancer and was ministering to other patients, his personality completely changed from that of a calculating ecclesiastic to that of a fellow human being.

In his last months of life, Cardinal Bernardin approached me during a bishops' annual meeting, which I was attending as a guest. He had learned of my mother's illness and her approaching death. Vestiges of resentment and anger that I had not yet resolved surfaced in my emotions as the cardinal drew near to greet me. Gaunt and slowed by the illness that would soon take his life, Cardinal Bernardin seemed very different from the person I had known when he was the president of the NCCB. His words of sympathy and friendship seemed more genuine. He was more focused and present and centered without the façade of earlier years. I was happy to see him comfortable in his own skin.

My disappointment over the divisions and political maneuvering that followed the bishops' bicentennial program gave way to my overriding sense of gratitude for the experience. Not only had I learned how church leadership and structures worked, but I also had gained a new appreciation for the public advocacy role of the Catholic Church for the voiceless in American society and elsewhere around the globe. The hierarchy's influence in matters of war and peace, human dignity, poverty, racial justice and immigration, and so many other issues constituting the common good is not inconsiderable. My years walking the halls of Congress on behalf of the bishops brought home that lesson.

So did traveling the country with Cardinal Dearden and other bishops confirm in me that manifold members of the Catholic community wish to be heard better and treated as coequal, baptized participants in the church's life and mission.

Looking back at those years at the USCC and the NCCB, I feel that my service there was a privileged gift and a necessary stage in my understanding of the church's leadership. It was a catalyst for growth and preparation for the amazing chapter that followed.

6

Growing FADICA

The retirement dinner was well attended at the Florida beachside resort. Nearly a hundred of my colleagues in FADICA (Foundations and Donors Interested in Catholic Activities), an association of Catholic philanthropists, were cheering when the organization's board chairman, Will Raskob, raised his glass in a toast. Thirty-three years had passed quickly since I left the Catholic bishops' conference to lead this organization. Now it was time to retire.

How could I adequately thank this audience that, for decades, had supplied generous support and creativity to bring about timely improvements in Catholic life? These changes included:

- A multimillion-dollar campaign to address the retirement needs of more than fifty thousand U.S. religious women and men
- A vast program of aid to rebuild the Catholic Church in eastern and southern Europe and Russia
- The seed funding for award-winning high schools for children of immigrants and low-income families
- A new resource to help dioceses and Catholic organizations use professional management and planning
- Adoption of more financial transparency in the business affairs of the Vatican

I thought of all these milestones while listening to Will light-heartedly joke about how exhausted everyone was after three decades of feverish activity and global travel.

It had been a long, fast-moving term, but one that held lessons for laypeople and anyone else interacting with Catholic organizations. Ours was a history of surprises, intrigue, providential alliances, and well-conceived grant making.

Here's how it began.

The phone on my desk at the United States Catholic Conference (USCC) rang persistently one summer afternoon in 1980, when everyone else seemed to be on vacation. I was trying to use this otherwise quiet time to edit the tenth draft of a committee's pastoral letter on racism. Very soon, a committee of bishops would meet to take up the paper, make changes, and move it for approval by all U.S. bishops.

I picked up the handset and realized that it was Peter Robinson calling, a friend whom Msgr. Geno Baroni, a well-known social activist in Washington, DC, had introduced to me four years earlier during the bicentennial program. Peter, a member of the Raskob Foundation of Wilmington, Delaware, had been working for Msgr. Baroni as a neighborhood policy analyst at the National Center for Urban and Ethnic Affairs. The National Conference of Catholic Bishops had contracted with him to compose an essay on neighborhoods for our parish-based discussions. Peter had done a fine job on the assignment, and I was grateful.

That particular day, Peter brought me up to speed on his current work as the head of a new philanthropic organization that his family had started, called FADICA. A few years earlier, I had been invited to address this organization on the subject of the Call to Action conference. The Raskob Foundation and the Frank J. Lewis Foundation had helped fund the travel of people unable to pay so that they could take part in the Detroit-based meeting.

But Peter's call was not about FADICA. He wanted my opinion about church research at CARA (the Center for Applied Research in the Apostolate), which was located in the nation's capital.

"This was Cardinal Cushing's brainchild," I said to Peter. The late Boston cardinal had proposed to American bishops that they should employ survey research data to make pastoral work more effective. Cushing formed the organization in the early 1960s.

"Cushing never mentioned who would pay for such research,"

I quipped, anticipating that Peter was about to say that his family wanted the U.S. bishops taking more responsibility for CARA's funding.

"No, it's more than the financial question," Peter responded. "My new board has some larger concerns about how research is used in the church. Would you have some time to talk with our members?" Then, pausing, he added, "Like, this afternoon?"

I looked at my watch and glanced at the marked-up draft sitting before me. A four-block walk to the Mayflower Hotel in the summer air would do me some good.

The CARA discussion turned out to be a ploy. FADICA did have a philanthropic interest in the research organization, but Robinson and his board raised an altogether different topic when I walked into their meeting a short time later.

Peter, FADICA's executive director, was leaving Washington with his wife, Anne, who had accepted a banking position in New York City. Peter had been offered a new job in New York helping a member of FADICA start up a new private foundation. I quickly realized that I was the focus of an executive search for Peter's successor to lead FADICA.

Peter smiled sheepishly while his board searched my face for a reaction. I was surprised. Here was an attractive opportunity to use my church-related background, but also a chance to escape the confines of ecclesiastical officialdom, which were wearing thin now that newer, younger, more conformist bishops were being appointed under John Paul II's papacy.

The job at FADICA would keep me in the world of Catholicism. Its connections to laypeople of wealth fired up my imagination about the potential of the group to make things happen.

"You've got great possibilities here, Frank," said John Bruderman, a Brown Brothers broker and founding board chairman of FADICA. John's straightforward manner suggested that the underlying vision of the group was one that complemented Cardinal Dearden's vision of laity and clergy, grounded in an equal baptismal dignity, working together to exercise their shared responsibility for the church.

"FADICA is not a church auxiliary," John said. "We are not even in the *Official Catholic Directory*," he added, to make his point. The *Official Catholic Directory* (ODC) was a big book authorized by the American bishops for groups and dioceses that had been officially recognized by the church. FADICA had wanted its independence and avoided inclusion in the book to obviate any oversight by the USCC's meddlesome lawyers.

A month later, I reported for work at the small FADICA office in downtown Washington. No one was there to welcome me; Peter Robinson had already departed for his new job as executive vice president for the just-created Brencanda Foundation in New York.

After working in an eighteen-person office, I had to adjust to the quiet solitude of FADICA. With no orientation and no game plan to review, I found the articles of incorporation, an annual audit, meeting minutes, and a bank statement. These dry documents constituted all there was of FADICA, but they were eye-opening.

It seemed that there was less of an organization than I had been led to think. Would something so small be able to do much?

I called Peter Robinson in New York, and he reassured me that the dozen or so members of FADICA would be supportive of the directions I would recommend.

Some weeks later, I understood what Peter was suggesting. He was now making funding decisions for Brencanda, and he was also an influential member of the Raskob Foundation, one of the oldest private foundations with Catholic interests. Peter himself could make things happen for FADICA.

Within a month, any worries I'd had about FADICA's survival subsided, and I was off to meet one of the original members, Harry John, the heir to the Miller Brewing fortune, who lived in Milwaukee and was known for his generosity and his eccentricities. Harry was the grandson of Frederick Miller, a German immigrant who made it big in the beer industry in Milwaukee. Nearly a century later, the bulk of the inherited Miller family wealth had been put into a foundation overseen by Harry and his wife, Erica, and two friends, Marquette University professors Donald and Idella Gallagher.

The foundation supported monasteries and convents and all

kinds of Catholic mission work across the globe. Its endowment had now grown to well over a hundred million dollars, making it among the largest of its kind in the world and a favorite destination of Catholic fundraisers.

As the years progressed, Harry's conservative outlook on the world took a sharply reactionary turn. Rather than promoting the renewal of the church called for by the Second Vatican Council, Harry became obsessed with maintaining a version of Catholicism that kept the ramparts up against the surging tide of secularism. It was a militant outlook I was familiar with, having encountered it within the American church hierarchy.

Up until my trip to Milwaukee, my encounter with people of wealth had been very limited. I had imagined very rich people to be like John Beresford Tipton Jr., the central character of the TV series *The Millionaire* that ran weekly in the 1950s of my childhood. Tipton, whose face the viewer never saw directly, was always seated in a comfortable Queen Anne armchair in front of a roaring fireplace in a well-appointed living room. On each episode, he would hand his secretary checks for a million dollars. They were to be given anonymously to average people whose lives would change for the better.

That was far from the scene I found when I arrived at the DeRance Foundation. The DeRance headquarters in suburban Milwaukee reminded me of a small police station. The receptionist, a smiling, older woman, confirmed that I was expected, but she informed me that I was to be photographed before I would be allowed to proceed. In these pre-9/11 days, I tried to hide my surprise. The receptionist politely explained, "Mr. John likes to keep a file on all his foundation petitioners so that he can recall them in the future."

With protocols completed, I was escorted to an expansive library, where Harry John and what looked like a brown-robed friar were in the middle of a heated exchange.

"Drink it!" commanded Harry. Green goo with a frothy head on it filled a Waring blender in Harry's right hand. "Drink it!" Harry demanded once more as the cowering friar's face turned crimson.

"I can't," the monk countered in faint protest.

"So, you won't, eh?" Harry scowled, as I looked on, embarrassed by the melodrama before me. Harry wore a T-shirt and black slacks with sandals and socks, while sporting a Marine's haircut.

"You chicken," Harry laughed, gulped down several ounces of the mysterious green slop, and slammed the blender back on its base.

"And who are you?" This question he directed at me, where I stood in the doorway wearing my neatly pressed business suit.

I handed him my card and explained the purpose of the visit. "Oh yeah," he said. "You are taking over for that Raskob fellow, right?"

Harry let out a big burp and shuffled past the friar.

"What's that you're drinking exactly?" I asked, in an effort to lighten the moment.

"This ungrateful friar doesn't appreciate all the vitamins and minerals I put together here to extend his life," answered Harry.

The monk disappeared back into a small office while Harry signaled for me to take a seat at a library table.

I began to explain how I had been offered this new position with FADICA. I was not sure that Harry was listening to anything I said because he kept checking his watch and looking out the window behind me.

"I don't think we are interested anymore in your organization," Harry announced.

I was speechless.

"Yes, we're done," he added, taking in the shocked look on my face. This was the largest Catholic foundation in the United States, and Harry was calling it quits for FADICA just as I was arriving.

He watched as I struggled for words. Then he smiled slightly and continued, "That is," he hesitated briefly, "unless you could help us identify the enemies of the Catholic Church."

By then I had regained a more stoic face. I told Harry, "No doubt there are enemies, but the mission of FADICA is a little more uplifting."

Harry rubbed the two-day stubble on his face and removed his glasses, then just stared off in the distance for half a minute.

I could hear the clock tick on his desk. I expected Harry to tell me to just hit the road.

"Let's have lunch," he said abruptly, laughing boisterously as he stood up, as though all of this was a big joke.

I was dealing with a true oddity. I needed everyone listed on FADICA's small membership list, eccentric or not. Harry's foundation underwrote Catholic projects all over the world. The board minutes of FADICA revealed that Harry was a founding member of my new group. I could not afford to write him off, so I was relieved to receive his invitation to lunch.

I followed Harry downstairs to the foundation's dining room, where we joined his wife, Erica, the professorial Gallaghers, and Harry's sidekick monk. We ate a hearty meal of corn on the cob, baked potatoes, and green beans, while Harry pontificated on the value of carbohydrates.

After lunch, a rumpled but kindly Don Gallagher invited me to visit with him in a nearby office. Dr. Gallagher, as he preferred to be called, kept things fairly formal. It was Mr. Butler and Mr. John. I learned from Gallagher that Patrick Riley, a former reporter for the conservative *National Catholic Register*, had joined the DeRance Foundation staff and that all of the foundation's previous grantees were being reviewed for their theological orthodoxy.

Gallagher said that Harry was increasingly more determined to redirect his charity to support more traditional groups and causes that were "faithful to the Magisterium."

This phrase was code that indicated not only a strict attitude toward religious teaching and moral behavior, but also a sign that you were on board with the then-two-year-old pontificate of Pope John Paul II.

"I am new to FADICA," I reminded Dr. Gallagher, "but I don't think that charitable groups like ours get very involved in matters of doctrinal orthodoxy."

"I am not saying that I agree with Mr. John," the professor interrupted. "I am only saying that everything seems to be under review here, so you will just have to wait and see if Mr. John continues his support."

I returned to Washington with the uneasy feeling that the organization I was asked to lead was somewhat of a fiction. Even its founding members were not very committed to its work, judging from my meeting with Harry John.

Ironically, Harry's more down-to-earth wife, Erica, would later join FADICA, become chair of its board of directors, and make major contributions to the association's programs.

Yet in the weeks that followed that visit to Milwaukee, more challenges ensued, as several other foundations failed to return calls. What was going on?

One afternoon, a phone call came from John Bruderman, the original board chair of FADICA and director for a small Belgian-based charity named the Robert Brunner Foundation. John thanked me for my decision to join the FADICA team. He asked how things were going.

I moaned slightly. "John, I would be less than honest if I told you that I was encouraged." "What's the problem?" he asked.

"Seems like the few members that I have interviewed are mostly on the fence about the whole FADICA experiment," I explained.

John's uncontrolled laugh puzzled me.

"What is this all about?" I was slightly agitated by his strange sense of humor.

"I should tell you about my own visit to the DeRance Foundation," John said. "It was like a set on a Fellini movie." He chuckled. "Lots of unusual characters and total confusion. Welcome to Catholic philanthropy, Frank."

John Bruderman encouraged me not to lose heart. He assured me that I had just the right background for what the board had in mind, or as he put it flatteringly, "a layperson with an advanced theological education, working contacts at high levels of the church, and a desire to help fellow Catholics work together to advance its mission."

"What could be a better choice?" John asked, as he promised his support and confidence. "We need you, Frank," he said, and ended the conversation to take another call.

Two weeks later, I was in Los Angeles to visit with a one-hundred-year-old Vincentian priest, the Reverend William G. Ward, CM, executive director of the Carrie Estelle Doheny Foundation.

The wealth of the foundation was generated by the long-deceased Edward Doheny, an oil baron, notorious for his involvement in the Teapot Dome scandal during the Harding administration in the early 1920s.

Then U.S. secretary of the interior Albert Fall had leased oil production rights to the Federal Elk Hills Oil Reserve to Doheny on very favorable terms in exchange for a no-interest loan by Doheny to Secretary Fall. Doheny was found not guilty, but Fall was convicted of bribery.

The Dohenys had long passed away, and the foundation had been entrusted to Fr. Ward's leadership. An early supporter of FADICA, the Doheny Foundation declined to renew its dues contribution to FADICA that first year after I arrived. I dropped in on Fr. Ward to ask why.

"It is nothing in particular, young man," whispered the frail Fr. Ward in the slightly high-pitched voice of an elder. "It is just that we have so many good causes and we can't support them all," he continued.

Probably out of sympathy for the long trip across the country I had just taken, Fr. Ward offered some hopeful advice. "Why don't you try us again in a few months?"

At that point, I knew I had to make an important decision. If the original founding members of FADICA were losing interest, I would have to either move to other work or buckle down and build up FADICA's membership.

I chose right then and there to start knocking on doors in search of Catholic foundations.

After the visit to Fr. Ward, I made some random calls to private family charities, where research had revealed some history of Catholic funding interests. The Thomas and Dorothy Leavey Foundation was one such charity, established by the cofounder of Farmers Home Insurance Company, Tom Leavey. The company started in downtown Los Angeles and aimed to give rural Americans less expensive home and auto insurance. Leavey died in the late 1970s and his wife, Dorothy, presided over the family's foundation. It had a history of support for Jesuit causes, especially Georgetown and Santa Clara Universities.

Dorothy Leavey's son-in-law, attorney Tom McCarthy, a personal injury lawyer and a convert to Catholicism, did the day-to-
day work of screening grantees and representing the foundation.
I reached Tom by phone, and to my surprise he agreed to listen
to a short pitch about FADICA. He invited me to his office later
that afternoon, housed atop one of the tallest buildings in downtown Los Angeles.

This suntanned California attorney was not the stereotype of a
power broker that I had anticipated. Tom's relaxed and welcoming
manor put me at ease. He was amiable and genuinely interested in
the fact that there were other Catholic-oriented foundations that
wanted to stay in regular touch with one another.

"So, let me see if I understand," said Tom. "This group is
about four years old. The Doheny Foundation has been a member, and when you meet it's to share information about Catholic
philanthropic projects?" Tom restated what he heard, like the
courtroom lawyer that he was. I nodded to indicate that he had
his facts in order.

"How would our philanthropy benefit from membership?"
Tom wanted to know.

I told him that his foundation would learn what its counterparts
were involved in and occasionally multiply its giving impact by
working with other foundations.

Tom seemed to appreciate how difficult it was for me to pitch
a group located on the East Coast that had such a small constitu-
ency, no track record of accomplishments so far, and an executive
who barely knew the world of philanthropy.

Tom said, "I'll let you know," as he patted me on the back and
shook my hand.

Later that afternoon, buoyed by Tom's warm reception, I drove
around the Los Angeles freeways, stopping at other foundation
offices to see whether I could get my foot in the door.

One of these was the Bob and Delores Hope Foundation,
located near one of the major movie studios in Hollywood.

I rang the front doorbell at what looked like a suburban house–
turned-office. A woman appeared behind opaque jalousies. She
curtly asked me what I wanted. I was searching for the Bob and

Delores Hope Foundation, I explained, and added that I represented an association of Catholic foundations called FADICA.

"We know about FADICA," she replied, surprising me to an almost startling degree.

"Could I take a moment of your time then?" I asked in a salesmanlike fashion.

"No, you can't," she crackled. "You can leave though."

"Sure was a challenge to get here." I interjected, hoping to stir sympathy.

"Go," she commanded.

I headed for my economy-size rental car. My new self-confident salesmanship seemed no match for this sentinel of Bob and Delores Hope. *How could she possibly know about FADICA?* I wondered as I backed out of the driveway looking both ways, expecting wailing squad cars to arrive any second.

Weeks later, the mystery of what I had encountered was resolved. I had unknowingly waded into a family feud. Delores Hope and Peter Grace, CEO of the shipping and chemical giant, Grace Company, were both well-known names in the world of Catholic philanthropy, especially in the 1960s. Delores's cousin Terrance Meehan was Peter Grace's chief of staff.

Peter's younger brother, Charles, with whom he often battled over the direction of the Grace Company, had become a supporter of FADICA during its first years.

Charles's involvement was a problem for Peter Grace, who had long-standing friendships with prominent families of wealth and had no tolerance for his younger brother's intrusion into a world that Peter considered his exclusive domain: church-related philanthropy.

The result translated into the firm rebuff that I had experienced on my first membership recruitment attempt. I was learning the hard way about how the preexisting and interlocking family relationships and alliances in Catholic philanthropy would shape the network that I sought to build.

Within an hour of what I have often called my escape from the Hope Foundation, I was on more friendly turf in the gleaming Century City office of Donald Hubbs, the attorney for the

Conrad N. Hilton Foundation. Hubbs had been a longtime friend and personal attorney of the late hotel magnate.

After Hilton's death the previous year, Hubbs helped establish the charitable foundation in Hilton's name. It was fast becoming one of the largest grant-makers in the entire nation. Throughout his life, Conrad Hilton supported global humanitarian aid, especially the work of Catholic sisters, whom Hilton befriended over his lifetime.

Because of this Catholic history, I thought that there might be a chance to sign up the Hilton Foundation as a new member of our association. As I sat down in his wood-paneled office, Don Hubbs informed me that he was not himself a Catholic. Nonetheless, I told him that Hilton should join FADICA because the contacts might come in handy when Hubbs needed third-party opinions about the foundation's future Catholic interests.

Hubbs listened politely but made no promises, and we said farewell.

I was optimistic. Despite its congestion and sprawl, I was finding Los Angeles a promising area. I had made unexpected headway in recruiting possibly two relatively new and very large foundations for FADICA.

Diligence, as the saying goes, seemed to be the mother of good fortune.

Months raced by into a first year. Before I knew it, positive decisions of the Leavey Foundation and Hilton Foundation to join FADICA jump-started a rapid expansion of the membership. Not only did we have more people in our network, but we were gaining a deeper bench of recruits for FADICA's board of directors. Those founding board members, lacking a dependable commitment to FADICA's growth, were gently rotated off, thanked, and replaced with more energetic and, in many cases, more resourceful people.

One such addition was a business leader from New York and a member of a large European family in the retail clothing business. Anthony Brenninkmeyer not only oversaw the family's businesses in the United States but he also chaired the Brencanda Foundation, where Peter Robinson, my FADICA predecessor and mentor, was now executive vice president.

In the tradition of European philanthropy, the Brenninkmeyers maintained a low profile. No buildings bore their name, and their charitable foundations required agreements to maintain the family's anonymity. Over decades, the Brenninkmeyer family had developed one of the most impressive social research and talent networks of any major philanthropy operating in the Catholic world. Moreover, some of its members were priests and sisters, providing the family with on-the-ground perspectives on church needs.

For the lay members of the family, the Brenninkmeyers discouraged the acceptance of invitations for board service on the charities they supported. Board membership meant greater visibility. Besides, the very large competitive retail enterprises that they managed kept family members on the move across the globe.

But I could tell from Anthony Brenninkmeyer's attendance at the FADICA conferences that he might be willing to make an exception to family policy in the case of our organization. He had an interest in scouting out talent in the Catholic Church in the United States, and we were regularly showcasing top-notch thinkers. Anthony also wanted to know more Catholic philanthropists who might wish to enter into funding partnerships.

With Peter Robinson's help, Anthony agreed to join the FADICA board. I was elated. I felt this to be another pivotal moment for the organization. It would open more doors for me to engage major philanthropists and link FADICA to the vast global grid of Catholic charitable endeavors that the Brenninkmeyers supported.

Fr. Bert Linders, a French Jesuit and high school teacher working in Egypt, was on that grid. Linders had benefited from the Brenninkmeyers' charitable support for Jesuit activities in the Middle East for many years. One day, this colorful, humorous, slightly built priest dressed in a well-worn polo shirt and jeans arrived at FADICA's door unannounced. He was on a global fundraising pilgrimage for the Holy Family School in Cairo. Each summer, Linders hitchhiked and took Greyhound buses throughout the United States, searching for donors who might be interested in supporting Jesuits teaching mostly poor Muslim children.

The casually dressed Linders introduced himself to me and established instant rapport with his self-deprecating humor. He told me that he had learned my name through the Brenninkmeyers.

Bert's knowledge of the Middle East and his wily ability to navigate its dangerous polarities were fascinating. He was a spell-binding analyst of Middle East politics and a dauntless fundraiser. Bert came to be a regular annual visitor. He would visit Wall Street, drop down the East Coast to Washington, and then proceed by bus for the long trek to Texas—all in an effort to ask for donations and to look for new donor leads.

In the course of his visits to FADICA, Bert suggested that I call one of his Wall Street friends who had been very generous to the Holy Family School. George Espy Doty was a managing partner at Goldman Sachs and the head of its administrative department. He was a legend at the investment bank and had helped it adopt rigorous rules on finances and conduct.

Doty was also a former chairman of the board of Fordham University, his alma mater, and known in Middle Eastern Christian circles as a guardian angel for good works of the Christian community there.

Bert warned me that Mr. Doty was all business and told me to be prepared to make the case for FADICA as free of any sales gibberish as possible.

Later that week I caught the shuttle to New York, after phoning Doty's office and mentioning Fr. Linder's name. I landed the appointment to meet the man Bert described as a tough-minded but very generous donor.

When I reached the Goldman Sachs headquarters across from the New York Stock Exchange, I sensed that I had entered the wealth zone of the world. I was fascinated by the frenzied vibe of fortune making before me as I killed time before my appointment by watching floor traders on the exchange yell arcane numbers and phrases in this pre-handheld computer era.

Even then, Goldman was one of the largest investment banks on the globe and managed the majority of mutual funds and hedge funds that existed. In the same year, Goldman was helping Microsoft go public and aiding General Electric as it sought to buy RCA. Goldman was the Mount Everest of money, and George

Doty was at the higher altitudes of the bank as a key director of its internal operations.

Mr. Doty's lavishly paneled offices had a spectacular view of the city. He did not smile when he extended a hand to greet me. His quiet politeness and the endless ringing of buzzers and phone lines suggested that I should get to the point as quickly as possible.

"Fr. Bert Linders urged me to meet you," I started. "He told me how much you've helped him," I went on, "and was aware that you were planning to devote more time to philanthropy." To my own ears, my comments were sounding a bit random in Doty's wildly paced day. "I just wanted to let you know about a group of Catholic donors who are meeting regularly and working together." Doty listened.

"We would welcome you to attend any of our meetings," I said, wanting to get to the point of the visit quickly. "It's a small group, but you might find our network and information-sharing helpful."

As I spoke, the electronic buzzers, flashing computer screens, and noise of unanswered phones just outside Doty's office door added to the cacophonous atmosphere.

"You might be familiar with some of our associates," I contin- ued, "like the Raskob Foundation of Wilmington," thinking the name might trigger some recognition of John J. Raskob's era on Wall Street. The builder of the Empire State Building and corpo- rate leader at the Dupont Chemical Company and General Mo- tors, Raskob was a legendary investor and Catholic philanthropist.

Doty took it all in without comment. I thought he would mention his involvement in the Middle Eastern charities that Fr. Linders had mentioned, or maybe even some of his interests in the Jesuit world. He said nothing.

There was no mention of the Doty endowed chair at Ford- ham, nor the list of playgrounds and children's charities all over Israel that he and his wife, Marie, had financed. He was not a self-promoter.

I seemed to be getting nowhere.

After a moment of awkward silence Doty finally spoke. "I don't have the time." he said. "Anyway," he asked sardonically, "why should I care what the Raskob Foundation may be doing? I have an endless stream of people coming by like Fr. Linders. I either like what they are doing or, if it is not my cup of tea, I take a pass. That's it." His tone was matter-of-fact.

With that, Doty stood up.

Nearly everyone I approached based their objections to joining FADICA on the excuse of adding administrative costs to their process of charitable giving—money, they argued, that could otherwise be given away to charities. It was a cogent argument but did not square oftentimes with the administrative waste of the charities that they listed on the foundation's tax forms. But with George Doty I heard no such objection to FADICA other than that membership would be time-consuming.

As I headed for the door, I pulled out some printed material on FADICA's next meeting and gently laid it on the corner of Doty's desk, wondering if he would be tempted to read it.

Still, I was fighting a gnawing annoyance at Doty's lack of curiosity or interest in meeting other donors, so I said impulsively, "The way you do your charity makes sense for most people. But for someone who is in the business of helping folks figure out good investments from not-so-good investments, I imagine you value as much research and opinion as you can find." I went on, somewhat surprised at my own nerve. "Of course, it takes time to do what our donors do," I said, moving closer to the door and trying not to sound impolite, "but so do all the things we value. We are meeting in two weeks in Scottsdale, Arizona, and you would be most welcome there," I said, still feeling as though the likelihood of Doty showing up was next to zero.

He walked me to the elevators, saying nothing except, "Thank you for stopping by," as the elevator doors opened, and I nodded farewell.

Weeks later, we were at an Arizona resort hotel where FADICA had gathered for a conversation with the president of the U.S. bishops, James Malone, the bishop of Youngstown, Ohio. To my great surprise, George E. Doty walked into the conference room.

Not only had he found the precise location of the meeting

from the material I left on his desk, but he took a seat as though he had been a member of FADICA for some time and joined right in our conversation with Bishop Malone.

George Doty brought the perspective of a well-informed, seasoned observer of the hierarchy. I was stunned by his knowledge and nuance. But most of all, I was shocked by his apparent change in thinking about his rugged individualist approach to philanthropy.

I later learned that speaking from the heart as I had that first day in his office impressed George. He confided years later that when I left his office that day, he could hear the refrain of Psalm 90 resonating: "If today you hear his voice harden not your hearts." And, in the spirit of his Jesuit formation, he took this scriptural passage as an invitation to something important.

We can't appreciate the mysterious ways that our words work. In this case, they were surely sourced in a world we cannot see yet interplays daily with the one we do see. Thus works the divine outreach through each one of us.

George would go on to help FADICA as a lead partner in history-making endeavors of the organization. He would become a close friend to several in the organization, and an invaluable mentor to me over many years.

With momentum building for new FADICA leadership, I tried my luck in Pittsburgh, tracking down a Catholic attorney and investor whose service on several volunteer boards suggested solid qualities of Christian leadership.

Thomas J. Donnelly was a good friend of Fr. William J. Byron, SJ, the first Jesuit president of the Catholic University of America, whom I greatly admired for his service and advocacy for the world's poor. Donnelly was not only on the CUA board but worked with Fr. Byron in the founding days of the Bread for the World campaign, an outstanding ecumenical effort to combat world hunger.

Orphaned as a child with two siblings, Tom had been raised by his maiden aunt, Mary. After his education and early law practice in the 1950s, Tom joined two high school classmates in founding Federated Investors, one of the first major mutual funds in the country.

After arriving at Tom's Pittsburgh office, I introduced myself and asked about the Mary J. Donnelly Foundation, a small fund that Tom managed. Tom explained the fund's range of interests, which were more than just local in scope and contained an impressive array of charities that I admired.

What seemed to interest Tom about my work was the fact that Catholic-oriented foundations had, on their own initiative, put together an independent network. Typically, Catholic organizations had bishops on their board. But not FADICA, Tom noted. Its independence from the control of church officials, like the members' family foundations themselves, was intentionally free from ecclesiastical politics, he noted, and he liked that very much.

As interested as Tom seemed in joining, he was overly conscious of the modest size of the Mary J. Donnelly Foundation's annual giving—in those days in the hundreds of thousands of dollars—considerably smaller than most FADICA members. Tom's lack of pretention and deep knowledge of the church confirmed the hunch I had that he would be a great FADICA board member. His fluent criticism about the underdeveloped voice of Catholic laity and his enthusiasm for the social mission of the church suggested that Donnelly would have much to add to FADICA's work.

Tom's parting question to me was, "Were you in the seminary?"

"I'm not wearing black shoes and pants anymore," I kiddingly replied. "How'd you guess?"

"Well," said Tom quickly, "your degrees and work experience were two big hints, but your Irish face confirmed it."

With the addition of Tom Donnelly, George Doty, and Anthony Brenninkmeyer, and the new memberships of the Hilton and Leavey Foundations, FADICA was gaining some serious thought-leader depth.

Another key addition about this time who brought both fun and an aura of quiet goodness was Philip D. Lewis: a playful, blustery southern politician in the tradition of Senator Beauregard Claghorn, a popular fictional character in the early days of broadcasting.

Phil, in addition to being a public servant, was a realtor. His brother Ed was a Palm Beach, Florida, attorney. They were the sons of Catholic donor Frank J. Lewis, a Chicagoan who made his fortune in the paving business, and later, Florida real estate. Frank J. Lewis helped found a technical university in his name and a Jesuit law school in Chicago as well as a national church funding agency for the rural U.S. dioceses called the Catholic Church Extension Society.

Though both Phil and Ed had known about FADICA from its beginnings, neither was active until I suggested that one or the other attend a FADICA conference on priestly and religious vocations. When Phil showed up at the Chicago hotel where we were meeting, I thought he was a conventioneer who had lost his way. He entered the room wearing a conventional sports jacket, slacks, shirt, and tie, but also what looked like a welder's helmet. Phil touched the device, and it sprang back on the top of his head. He extended his hand to me with a smile, pointing to the welder's facemask and adding, "It helps when I get a migraine."

The topic of priestly vocations was of great importance to Phil. But as he introduced himself, no one seemed to be listening. People only stared at the welder's helmet and Phil's unusual tie clip protruding beyond his suit coat. It was a working compass and bobbled when he turned his body in any direction.

We were in the presence of a man highly experienced in leaving a lasting impression. Lewis was an expert in mnemonic psychology. The more made-to-order one's personal image, the more voters would likely remember the candidate at election time.

Phil was a remarkably popular politician. President of the Florida State Senate, he was known as "Mr. Fix-It" in Florida politics, producing huge dividends for the state's infrastructure of highways, public safety, and educational institutions. Phil's public service opened the way for Florida to become one of the most populous states in the union.

But even more impressive was Phil's passionate advocacy for and personal involvement with homeless men and women. He looked after drifters who wandered by his real estate office, making sure that they had something to eat and a place to rest.

"If you want something done, ask a busy person," was never truer than in Phil Lewis's case. Over time, Phil would turn out to be one of our most conscientious and caring board leaders. He managed to juggle his many civic, family, and volunteer responsibilities with joy and genuine love for those he encountered.

Phil's eventual addition to the FADICA board, and the magic of his family's name in Catholic history, enabled the organization to take on catalytic potential to influence church leadership while it went about its work educating foundation leaders. This had practical benefits for philanthropy, amplifying its funding impact.

With a charitable capacity propelled by 180 dioceses and eighteen thousand parishes, Catholic bishops oversaw annual charitable revenues in the billions of dollars. A new affluence and the rising social status of American Catholic laity made that possible. This new social reality was not well appreciated by many bishops and pastors, who still considered their people to be striving, working-class Americans.

Leaders in Catholic universities and charities had a better understanding of the economic stature of Catholics. They were seeing the grandsons and granddaughters of poor immigrants now stepping up to build billion-dollar endowments, and succeeding at it.

With Catholic wealth and social standing vastly improving in the closing decades of the twentieth century, there was an emerging opportunity for Catholic donors to be more than passive spectators of the church. The Second Vatican Council articulated a theology that gave equal standing to clergy and laity through sacramental baptism. That spiritual framework seemed providential in dovetailing with the prosperity and high educational attainments of lay Catholics.

But greater donor involvement in the church would require changes in the traditional way that the church conducted its business. With its bright board leadership, FADICA set about influencing fundraising behavior to help the church awaken to changing attitudes on accountability and transparency.

One of the most shocking chapters in the financial history of the Vatican unfolded in the 1980s when a bank in Italy, with deep and extensive Catholic connections, went into bankruptcy.

The chairman of the failed Banco Ambrosiano was found dead under mysterious circumstances. Eventually, investigators found their way to the Vatican's bank, the IOR (Institute for the Works of Religion), whose principals were implicated in Banco Ambrosiano's financial crash. The bank creditors charged that the IOR played a role in a fraud scheme that caused the Milan-based bank to fail. The bankruptcy damage was in the billions of dollars. The IOR, while never admitting to fraud, nevertheless made a $240 million payment to the bank's creditors in what was euphemistically termed a "goodwill gesture."

With headlines about the scandal plastered across newspapers globally, it was a good time for the emergent FADICA to weigh in on the issue of openness in the church's handling of money. In 1986, at the urging of the board members, we planned the first Rome-based convening of our rapidly growing membership. It was time to introduce ourselves to the Vatican and open a conversation on charitable fundraising.

Arrangements were made to house philanthropists at the Excelsior Hotel near the U.S. Embassy. Each day for a week, we went by chartered bus to the Vatican. Small teams of FADICA members divided up to visit the dicasteries, or major Vatican offices. Later in the day, we reconvened at our hotel to share information on what each team had learned.

One team had met with Slovenian cardinal Jozef Tomko and learned how the poorer dioceses of the world received financial help from the Vatican's Congregation for the Evangelization of Peoples. The congregation received its funds from parishes throughout the world and functioned as a redistribution center so that very poor dioceses could afford to run seminaries or catechetical programs.

Another team visited the now notorious IOR bank and posed blunt and challenging questions to U.S. archbishop Paul Marcinkus, its governor, about his role in the Banco Ambrosiano affair. The archbishop was cordial but tight-lipped.

All of us were becoming familiar with the Vatican. Distressingly, we were piecing together a picture of financial ill health for the overall operations of the Holy See. Some thirty years of operating deficits were taking their toll. Cardinals seemed worried about growing payrolls and stagnant revenues. Looming over the whole institution was the Banco Ambrosiano scandal and the recent payment to its creditors—from funds reportedly set aside for future retiring Vatican employees.

I could tell from the grim atmosphere that we were not going to be allowed to leave Rome without some kind of fundraising request. It materialized one afternoon toward the end of our visit.

Cardinal Giuseppe Caprio, president of the Economic Prefecture, was among a group of officials to whom U.S. archbishop John Foley, our host, had introduced FADICA after a tour of the Pontifical Commission for Social Communications, which Foley directed.

The ornate offices of the commission were just behind St. Peter's Basilica and, history indicated, within a few yards of the execution site of St. Peter himself.

Cardinal Caprio, in heavily accented English, welcomed all of us gathered there and then urged us to remember the needs of the Holy See in what he called "these difficult days."

I did not expect much of a response to Caprio's soft-selling approach. It was generally met with polite silence by the thirty-five-member FADICA audience—some of whom could have moved the economic needle in a favorable direction had they been interested. Then one of the directors suddenly rose to his feet and declared, "No one here will pour money down a rat hole."

It was Tom Donnelly speaking. He startled everyone seated in the palatial marble-lined conference room. A stunned assembly of prelates wearing red zucchettos looked at one another in confusion.

"Tana del topo?" Cardinal Caprio asked Tom, thinking that he had misunderstood our translator.

"Yes, 'rat hole,' Your Eminence," Tom assured him. "We've never seen an accounting of church donations that you use here at the Vatican, and now we read of this awful banking scandal in Milan," Donnelly fumed. "On top of that, the people here expect us to believe the fiction that the Holy See has no connection to the IOR. I, for one, don't buy it," Tom declared, sounding like the trial attorney that he was.

The face of the cardinal was beginning to match the red satin buttons of his cassock.

"Tell you what though," Tom added, "if you'd be willing to provide more transparent financial information, we might be more inclined to talk with you further about your economic situation." Members all around the table held back their urge to laugh as several repeated the phrase "Tana del topo" to one another.

The next day, we were instructed to head for a private audience hall under the papal apartments for a meeting with Pope John Paul II.

We heard no further words about the financial needs of the Vatican, only praise for forming a lay organization devoted to charity.

John Paul offered words of encouragement and spoke of the spirit of collaboration underlying FADICA. It was the perfect endorsement to help put the group on the ecclesiastical map and allow doors to be opened in the future. It was also the first of several times we would meet with this future saint.

The Rome visit introduced FADICA to church officialdom at the highest level. It left images of U.S. Catholic donors as friendly, self-confident, and street smart, thanks in large part to Tom Donnelly's candor. These were not sheepish donors who could be patted on the head in the hope that they would open their checkbooks.

FADICA was off to a good start. But a huge challenge remained: to push further for whatever financial reforms we could manage within the Vatican. That would take some additional time—and alignment of the stars.

7

Everything under Control?

After our return to the United States, we continued to chip away at the issue of financial transparency in the church. But a more urgent crisis was unfolding. We in FADICA had been agents behind disturbing headlines.

In May 1986, the *Wall Street Journal* published a front-page story titled "Sisters in Need" by John J. Fialka, a skillful investigative reporter and devout fan of Catholic sisters.

Instantly, television networks and news outlets across the country picked up on Fialka's breaking story of older sisters living on the edge of bankruptcy in their final years due to the low wages they received teaching in parochial schools and the lack of any meaningful support for their retirement.

Bishops were stonewalling the leadership of religious women and men. The hierarchy refused to acknowledge their responsibility for the mounting financial burden of aging sisters and religious-order priests and brothers.

A year before the *Journal*'s story, Fordham University's Third Age Center, run by Msgr. Charles Fahey, and the Brencanda Foundation, under Peter Robinson's direction, had convened a retreat in Staten Island, New York. The retreat, which I attended as FADICA's representative, worked out a national strategy for what was fast becoming a multibillion-dollar nightmare. The meeting included some of the sharpest administrative minds in religious life.

The plan that the group devised involved organizing a fund-raising collection in the nation's eighteen thousand parishes and establishing a centralized office in Washington, DC, to redistribute collection proceeds to religious communities and provide them with technical support. But it went further, to the very source of the problem: the underpaying of religious.

The prevailing practice of paying stipends—and not full salaries—to religious women and men had to be scrapped, according to experts. The old system, based on concerns about paying people who lived under vows of poverty, had been adopted in a vocations-rich era when younger members of religious communities provided the care for their elderly retired members. This was no longer possible.

For nearly a century, the institutional growth of Catholicism in the United States was possible only because religious women and men were willing to donate their labor and service in a vast network of parish schools and charities. For example, in the 1950s and 1960s, many sisters were paid about fifty dollars per month. Parishes supplied a convent and school building, and often a modest budget for food for the religious teachers who served them. But almost nothing was left over from their monthly stipends to send back to the motherhouse for the community's mission or for retirement needs.

The system was exploitative, yet religious were bighearted. Younger religious continued to fill the ranks and provide what care was needed for retiring members.

That era ended in the early 1970s when the reservoir of Catholic vocations dried up essentially overnight. From then on, congregations of religious faced a costly and unanticipated future.

A gigantic unpaid retirement liability could not have come at a more inopportune moment. Dioceses themselves were feeling the impact of human resource shortages, with the vocation declines measured in the emptying of seminaries and convents. When the necessity of paying more lay salaries came into full swing in the early 1970s, it was altogether more expensive to sustain a giant and aging church infrastructure.

With the Staten Island retirement plan in hand, Sister Frances Mlocek, IHM, the chief financial officer for the U.S. bishops' conference and one of the brainpowers behind the Brencanda gathering, went to work to convince the bishops to face the music and consider the proposals that emerged from the Brencanda Foundation gathering.

Almost immediately, Sr. Fran met stiff resistance. She was told by United States Catholic Conference (USCC) leadership that the Staten Island event lacked official church standing and that its recommendations were simply some among the many possible ways of approaching the retirement problem.

Weeks went by until the discouraged Sr. Fran was contacted by Bishop John McGann of New York, whose sister was an influential woman religious. Bishop McGann, the treasurer for the USCC, said that he would review the Staten Island plan and do what he could to place it before his USCC Finance Committee.

It was a step in the right direction. I called the General Secretary of the USCC, Msgr. Daniel Hoye—a Fall River, Massachusetts, native—to convey thanks for this positive development.

"Look, Frank, I'll be honest with you," said the young Msgr. Hoye. "Most of the bishops are not keen on another parish-based nationwide collection."

"I'm not surprised," I responded. I was familiar with national parish fundraising collections, often referred to as "second collections," because they were supplemental to the main offertory collection, which usually paid for each parish's operating expenses. The second collections, managed for the most part by the USCC, processed over a hundred million dollars annually in grassroots support for a variety of charities, ranging from antipoverty work to Catholic seminaries.

Few Catholics were clear about these appeals, and fewer still had received an accounting of what happened to contributions made to them.

"But there's some good news," Hoye continued. "The plan that you and your religious friends proposed in Staten Island might ultimately be an exception to normal opposition to new collections. The bishops have no budget to get a national retirement office off the ground," he said. "Would your rich friends be willing to prime the pump with a year or two of start-up funding?"

"It can't hurt to ask," I told Hoye.

But Hoye had saved some hard news until now. "I don't think that bishops and pastors are suddenly going to start paying full salaries to religious," he said.

This was in reference to the Staten Island meeting's most controversial finding: salaries for religious were subpar, and that needed to be changed. The idea was dead on arrival according to Hoye and, in his judgment, would likely impede further progress on the other recommendations.

I weighed Hoye's words. If I pushed back on the compensation question, the whole project was in jeopardy. Bishops liked the cheap labor of religious, justifying their position by citing the vow of poverty. But it was precisely low compensation that landed religious in their present retirement predicament.

"Well, let's start with what we can agree on," I suggested to Hoye, without pushing the compensation off the table, "and that seems to be this national office. I will find your start-up funds."

The fight for just compensation would have to be revisited by religious themselves. Here at least was an opening to link religious to Catholic parishes across the land, and that meant new revenue of a considerable size that could be put to work helping elderly religious.

That week, I was able to raise from our FADICA members the $330,000 needed by the bishops' conference to start the National Office for Religious Retirement. The newer members of FADICA were united in their support of the idea of helping Catholic sisters in particular, and they made my promise to Hoye an easy one to fulfill. The Leavey and Hilton Foundations, which would go on to lead additional efforts to mobilize widespread interest in the sisters' retirement cause, were among the first to step up and help get the retirement project off the ground.

The governing board of bishops told Hoye to proceed with establishing the new national office and to launch a search for a director.

Months went by, and we began a new year, but still no word on Hoye's luck in opening the new office for religious retirement. Funds had been awarded to the USCC for this purpose through FADICA, yet the talent search for a director was as slow as molasses.

A midwinter meeting of FADICA's board came and went, and

suspicions were beginning to grow among FADICA's directors that the bishops were dragging their feet to avoid asking their parishes for the funds required.

"What's your plan now?" wondered Denise Hattler, chair of the Loyola Foundation, as a dozen FADICA members looked on. We were attending FADICA's annual meeting in a Florida hotel aside the glittering cobalt blue of the Gulf of Mexico.

"Denny," as she was known to us, was a devoted friend to scores of Catholic sisters because of her Manhattanville College roots with the Sacred Heart Community, a group known for its strong leadership.

Long ago, Denny had lost patience with church officialdom when the well-being of women was at issue. "Time to start educating the public," she declared.

Reaching Catholics in the parish without the USCC would be nearly impossible. The hierarchy had a monopoly on the Catholic press, and the story of nuns and religious in retirement arrears might seem of interest only to accountants and lawyers.

How was I to respond to Denny's suggestion? I kept thinking about it.

The Catholic bishops were at that time writing a pastoral letter on the U.S. economy. Their message would be titled *Economic Justice for All*. Such periodic declarations were issued by the bishops as joint teaching exercises. They seldom reached most people in the pew, but occasionally they shaped public opinion in Washington and managed to influence policies of the vast network of Catholic institutions.

At this time, however, Ronald Reagan was president, and the economy was growing at an annual rate of 2.5 percent, held back by a soaring trade deficit and the worst stock market performance in four years. The slowdown was taking its toll on lower wage earners and people on the margins of U.S. society.

The bishops intended to lift up the principles of Catholic social teaching and remind titans of industry and government of the principles of human solidarity, justice, and fairness. But what seemed missing in this episcopal exercise was a forthright application of these very same social principles within Catholic institutions themselves. A pastoral letter on the economy was being written, and public hearings by the bishops on their draft statement were under way. The *Wall Street Journal* had attacked the bishops' new document as anticapitalist and smugly hypocritical.

Within this highly charged setting I approached John Fialka to join me for lunch; this was months before his famous exposé on retired sisters.

I had dropped the name of a mutual friend and journalist, Jim Castelli, when I made the call. John was receptive to further discussion on the subject of justice and church compensation. He and I met at the Iron Gate Inn, a small restaurant tucked away in an alley behind St. Matthew's Cathedral in downtown Washington.

John normally reported on defense issues for the Pentagon, but he was also known for his insatiable curiosity and often colorful offbeat stories. I knew from Jim that Fialka had a strong Catholic background. He was raised in Iowa, attended Catholic schools, including Georgetown University, and had known plenty of sisters over his lifetime.

Over lunch, we talked about the Catholic Church and my professional background as a former advisor to bishops and now to wealthy Catholics. I shifted the conversation back to John's Catholic roots. He talked at length about his gratitude to the sisters who had taught him.

This was my opening to introduce John to survey research that FADICA had underwritten by priest-researcher Eugene Hemrick of Catholic University, documenting the religious retirement picture nationally.

Fialka was stunned to learn that the median age of the then seventy thousand Catholic sisters had reached sixty-two. But he was even more shocked to hear that there was so little provision for the retirement years of these women.

As we talked, John kept scribbling on a napkin. A story seemed to be taking form right in front of me.

"Most of the solution," I told him, "rests on the shoulders of every Catholic who ever benefited from a Catholic grade-school education or was born or treated with the help of a nurse-sister in a hospital."

"I think that there is a story here," John said softly, looking into a crackling restaurant fireplace. I guessed that he was recalling his parochial classroom back in Iowa where sisters helped him discover a love for writing.

An interested and influential journalist on this story—this was just what was needed to get the USCC to open the new national retirement office.

John and I exited the now empty restaurant. As John put on his coat, I said, "If you have any trouble with your editors at the *Journal*, remind them of the bishops' economic pastoral letter."

Fialka laughed. I had imagined the editors' delight when they discovered that the finger-wagging bishops might be over a barrel when the *Journal* exposed the injustice of these exploitative labor practices.

In the weeks that followed, John and I got to know each other through daily phone calls. I supplied the names of religious superiors and financial experts and shared research data that helped him in his own investigative work.

By mid-May, Fialka shared a draft of his story with me. It was titled "Sisters in Need: Are Bishops Evading a Responsibility to Help?" The story succinctly captured the actuarial nightmare.

Four days later, the article ran on the front page of the *Journal*. It caused a major uproar. Almost every print and electronic news media outlet was suddenly assigning reporters to stories of convent hardships.

The U.S. bishops' conference was predictably in a pickle. Not only was the USCC swarming with reporters eager to present the hierarchy in a hypocritical light, but thousands of readers across the country were expressing their shock over the neglect and unfairness that the news stories described.

Within days following publication of the *Wall Street Journal*'s revelations, John and I attended a press conference together at the USCC's downtown Washington headquarters on Massachusetts Avenue.

To the surprise of many present, the general secretary of the conference, Msgr. Hoye, introduced a Notre Dame sister, Mary Oliver Hudon, academic dean at the College of Notre Dame in Baltimore. She was to be the first director of the new Office for Religious Retirement, Hoye announced. The gray-templed sister took the microphone to answer questions from the press and to quell the uproar of shouting journalists.

"There is no crisis," declared the telegenic Sr. Mary Oliver. "No one is going to starve," she assured the press, seeking to calm the room.

The new appointee has some homework to do, I thought. Instead of using the occasion to mobilize the public concern further and prepare the ground for an eventual fundraising campaign, Sr. Mary Oliver spun the story in the best tradition of chancery apologists, suggesting that the press had barged in on a family discussion that was far from a crisis stage.

"Guess it's all under control," John whispered to me sotto voce as he shook his head in disbelief.

Within days, both of us were spending most of our work hours answering calls from around the country from people who had read John's story and wanted to help the sisters. While I was sending them to the new national office for retirement, Sister Mary's efforts to calm the storm of public opinion left me wondering whether she was just another paper-shuffling apologist for the bishops. I was beginning to entertain doubts that the Office for Religious Retirement would capitalize on the public awareness and sympathy for older religious.

John Fialka shared my misgivings. We discussed other challenges as well. For example, if the new retirement office coordinated a national parish-based appeal, large sectors of potential donors not connected to the Catholic Church could be missed because they did not attend Mass in parishes.

Should we try to start an additional charity that might cover these gaps?

John's career had put him in touch with a full range of entrepreneurs, including one of the founders of the Vietnam War Memorial, former Army captain Jack Wheeler, the memorial's first chair.

"How did you start national fundraising?" Fialka asked Wheeler days later, as the three of us sat down to lunch at the Mayflower Hotel early that summer.

You could discern a Texan twang in Wheeler's words. He was now serving as an attorney for the Securities and Exchange Commission in Washington. Wheeler had a reputation for brains and grit; he had taken on billionaire Ross Perot over the design of the veterans' memorial—and won.

"I'm not Catholic," Wheeler said respectfully, "but I do know that nuns do amazing work. I was damned sorry to read John's story about their present predicament. The main thing," he said, "is to ask yourself: *How committed am I to helping solve this problem?*" He looked at both of us and stopped for a moment for effect. Then he asked, "Do you think this crisis will be solved somehow regardless of what you two do?"

Neither John nor I said anything. I was thinking, *I am getting in too deep here.*

John broke the silence. "Let's assume that our involvement matters," he said to Wheeler.

"Then here is what you two do," Wheeler responded. "Ask for God's blessing," he bellowed out in the middle of a busy hotel restaurant in Washington. Then Wheeler grabbed one hand from each of us and led us in a revival-like supplication for Catholic sisters.

There we were, a reporter, a government worker, and a non-profit executive with our hands clasped together while suited men and women turned their heads and listened to Wheeler invoke the Holy Spirit for "valiant Christian ladies in their time of need."

"Tell you what," Wheeler added after praying. "When you leave here, call back everyone who called you about John's *Wall Street Journal* story. Let them know right now that you're about to start a charity to save aging sisters and you're meeting here in Washington on such-and-such a date and tell them to be there."

I had the feeling that aging sisters were about to become a big part of my life.

Over the following week, John and I phoned everyone who

had called us previously. More than a hundred of those people came to Washington weeks later for our charity formation event.

On a Saturday meeting at the Trinity College (now Trinity Washington University) auditorium in Washington, DC, the readers of John's article came together from across the country and designed and named a new charity to raise funds for the retirement needs of American religious. It was a barn-raising event that brought to life Support Our Aging Religious, known by its acronym, SOAR! The new charity operated out of FADICA's office for its first months. Denny Hattler's Loyola Foundation provided SOAR! its first big grant of a half million dollars to get the charity off the ground. Denny generously agreed to chair its first board of directors and was instrumental in drawing the interest of hundreds of people to the plight of elderly religious.

For the next three decades and to this day, SOAR! has gone on to award millions of dollars to help hundreds of religious congregations build elevators, furnish retirement facilities, pay heating bills, and otherwise meet the emergency retirement-related needs of Catholic sisters, priests, and brothers.

SOAR! also provided a catalyst for national parish-based fundraising under the National Retirement Office, which, soon after its founding, became operational with a nationwide yearly parish collection that continues to be the largest in the Catholic Church in the United States.

The combined efforts of the National Retirement Office and SOAR! have generated significant new resources—some eight hundred million dollars to date—for American religious communities of men and women. These resources have been put to work to help their older members live out their years in dignity and respect.

For too long, the expression "Everything is under control" has kept Catholicism from grappling head-on with serious challenges. These efforts on behalf of retired religious show the resourcefulness and untapped talent of ordinary Catholics to help their church solve practical problems that sadly are often kept out of sight.

8

Fostering Transparency
at the Vatican

While the start-up of SOAR! required FADICA's time and atten-tion, FADICA's visit with Pope John Paul II and his Curia advisors prompted church officialdom to talk with FADICA further about the Vatican's own financial plight.

Our 1986 visit to Rome opened our eyes to the fact that the Vatican lacked anything close to public standards of financial disclosure. Many of its financial and management structures were mysterious sinecures with their own stashes of funds that caught little accounting sunshine. The overall financial picture seemed even beyond the understanding of those in charge. The Vatican was long overdue for a good audit.

After FADICA returned from its frank exchange with papal advisors, its board of directors asked me to meet with the papal representative in Washington, DC, Archbishop Pio Laghi, and con-tinue to press the case for a "management study" of the Vatican's finances. We deliberately avoided the term "independent certified audit" because we had learned from our visit that this term would be a nonstarter in any conversation. Important voices within the Holy See insisted that an independent audit by an outside entity was not compatible with the Vatican's sovereignty as a nation-state.

I would often write to Archbishop Laghi and then stop by his stately embassy on Massachusetts Avenue's Embassy Row opposite the U.S. vice president's house in northwest Washington. "Yes, Dr.

Butler, we so appreciate your offer of help," Laghi would always say, then adding in a voice of urgency, "The Vatican needs all the assistance donors can provide!"

Then he would listen politely to a brief reiteration of FADICA's Rome visit and offer feigned assurances that someday our wishes to help might fall on receptive ears. We would shake hands, bid farewell, and then during the months that followed, nothing happened. So, like the movie *Groundhog Day*, I would call the delegate's number for another appointment, and another kabuki dance would follow.

Until one day a wonder occurred.

After hosting a well-executed visit of Pope John Paul II to heavily Polish Detroit in 1987, it was only a matter of time before Cardinal Edmund Szoka, the archbishop there, known for his grasp of church finance and tough management style, would be summoned to Rome to help improve its financial disorder.

Szoka received the red hat of a cardinal from John Paul II, and soon thereafter he was appointed to lead the Economic Prefecture, the closest thing to a comptroller in the Vatican organization.

I had known the cardinal from my work as a board member of the Catholic Telecommunications Network of America (CTNA), which Szoka chaired for the short lifespan of this bishop-sponsored experiment in cable outreach. Szoka was hard-nosed and stern, but his reputation for understanding numbers was vastly stronger than most of his brother bishops. Despite his facility for balancing the books, however, CTNA bit the dust under his leadership because his fellow bishops refused to supply the investment needed to compete in an explosive marketplace for cable television.

Before Cardinal Szoka departed for his new assignment as the pope's chief internal auditor, I invited him to lunch at the Detroit Athletic Club and brought with me four key FADICA board members: Tom Donnelly, George Doty, Anthony Brenninkmeyer, and Erica John. We intended to make the case for what we were calling our independent management study in the Vatican.

"I don't know what I am facing," the cardinal shared with the group in a warm, companionable gathering. "I am told that the

[Economic Prefecture] office has one Radio Shack computer and a sister who is of retirement age," he told us. "So I can't make any promises until I know more. But let me say now, I'll use your very welcomed help after I get the lay of the land."

Cardinal Szoka called me from Rome a few weeks later to say that he was anxious to get moving. He needed consultants in the auditing field and tech sectors to build his prefecture into "a first-class auditing operation."

George Doty, now FADICA's board treasurer, was the first on my list to call after Szoka's contact. Within a day, George had enlisted the expertise of William Schreyer, his friend and Merrill Lynch chairman, and with warplike speed Schreyer offered to donate on a pro bono basis two full-time executives from Merrill Lynch to work at the Vatican for the next few months and help Cardinal Szoka move forward.

Within eight weeks, Cardinal Szoka had introduced the Merrill Lynch volunteer executives to the principal reporting agencies under him, and they framed a proposal for a redesigned auditing capability for the prefecture.

The Economic Prefecture had been established in the early 1970s under Pope Paul VI to oversee financial reporting for the Holy See, but it had been ineffectual from its very outset. The office did not even possess the authority to report on the infamous Vatican bank, for example, nor did it have much clout with those many offices and operations that reported to the Vatican City state government.

Entrenched officeholders at the Holy See understood that Cardinal Szoka's obscure prefecture had no real firepower when it came to sanctions. Therefore, few cooperated with the prefecture's requests for financial reporting.

Cardinal Szoka, with the strong personal support of and ethnic ties to Pope John Paul II, was about to change all of that. Szoka's Merrill Lynch consultants returned to the States after several busy months. At George Doty's request, we planned a lunch at the Willard Hotel in Washington to see what further assistance Cardinal Szoka needed. I assembled the same FADICA team—Doty,

Donnelly, Brenninkmeyer, and John—who had accompanied me weeks before on our first visit with Szoka.

The Merrill Lynch executives were straightforward. They said that Cardinal Szoka needed nearly a half million dollars to equip his new auditing office with state-of-the-art computers that could be connected in real time throughout the Vatican to monitor and control spending.

It was a princely sum. I thought about the weeks or months it might take to raise it.

But after hearing the presentation, George Doty pulled out a blank check from his coat pocket and made it payable to FADICA for one hundred thousand dollars. The other donors watching George immediately signaled that they would join him, and within a few minutes, lickety-split, the needed funds had all been raised.

There was no hemming or hawing. No one said, "Well, I'll have to check with the other members of my foundation board." Like Doty, this group was all action. They realized that Szoka was sticking his neck out in trying to strengthen his prefecture. Support was essential to his success.

Cardinal Szoka moved rapidly forward with the redesign of the Holy See's auditing office. Only months later it had the capacity to provide a financial picture of the Holy See far more complete than at any time in its past.

The former Detroit archbishop pushed back against a hostile Curia, convincing Pope John Paul II that without a more credible financial reporting system, voluntary contributions from the world's dioceses would not improve. Word spread within the Vatican that Cardinal Szoka had rich friends in the States and that they were interested in management improvements.

As Cardinal Szoka's voice grew within the Curia, Cardinal Rosalio Jose Castillo Lara, a Venezuelan Salesian priest who headed up the principal administrative offices for the Holy See known as the APSA (Administration of the Patrimony of the Apostolic See), contacted the FADICA office. He asked for a meeting while he was in New York on investment-related business.

In view of his position as manager of the day-to-day operations of a substantial segment of the Vatican, including its commercial enterprises, the cardinal wanted to explore FADICA's interests in management studies.

I gathered our same donor team. This time we met at the Union Club in Manhattan, where Cardinal Castillo Lara joined us for a meal and conversation. Cardinal Castillo Lara seemed well briefed by Cardinal Szoka. Castillo Lara recited a brief laundry list of the Vatican's day-to-day challenges, including duplicative accounting systems, rising operational costs, and clerical resistance to new technology. He welcomed our interest and advice.

After several years of fruitless visits with the Vatican's representative in Washington, things were changing quickly. We were now the ones invited to listen. Within a month, we engaged management consultants in Italy to help Castillo Lara develop a project that could be undertaken right away and might also improve management and the bottom line of a Vatican entity.

We did not expect that the conversations with Castillo Lara would lead to a grocery store, but there it was: a company store for Vatican employees. It was losing money, and the cardinal asked for help.

Because of the modest salaries paid to the five thousand Vatican workers, popes historically provided a place where their families could shop and find lower prices than offered in the city of Rome. Products were not taxed by the Vatican and were duty free.

Nonetheless, despite its competitive advantage, the Vatican's employee store still had been losing customers to the large discount grocers in Rome that offered convenience, better hours, higher-quality merchandise, and most importantly, parking.

Our professional consultants surveyed employees and customers of the store and found their top complaint to be: *Nessun posto dove parcheggiare!* (There is no place to park!).

There were other problems too. A wide gap existed between what employees shopped for and what was actually available on store shelves. Checking out of the Vatican commissary was something out of the 1950s, as products lacked bar codes and cash registers were dated. Store employees did not have a good grasp of how to balance their inventory with customer demand.

Cardinal Castillo Lara wanted a complete overhaul of the store, so FADICA again supplied a great deal of the funding that enabled Rome-based consultants to coach the commissary staff in the thorough refitting.

Computerization was introduced. New systems would allow inventory to be resupplied from vendors without costly storage fees. A new parking lot was constructed for easier access, and items such as meat products, which ranked toward the top of consumer preference, received more commissary space.

Pope John Paul II thanks FADICA board member Anthony Brenninkmeyer during a visit to Rome in 1991. Looking on is Frank Butler, FADICA's president (Credit: Arturo Mari)

New lines of merchandise to help the Vatican realize a higher profit margin were suggested, such as the sale of electronics: televisions, cameras, and computers.

The renewal of Cardinal Castillo Lara's commercial enterprise resulted immediately in an improvement in revenues and cost savings in the millions of dollars. Moreover, with Szoka's eventual promotion to the post of governor of Vatican City, the duty-free shopping offered to Vatican employees was greatly expanded and generated a substantial source of new income.

But management improvement remained more a dream than reality, and huge amounts of papal influence were needed over a sustained period of years in order to clean up the financial chicanery, management incompetence, and downright corruption at work at Catholicism's headquarters. Financial scandals would continue to plague the Vatican for decades.

We did feel that getting our foot in the door to push for better management had been historic and unexpectedly fruitful. It marked a step toward a more financially accountable church and proof that a proactive change is possible if prior relationships are in place, and if dogged persistence guides the effort.

The dynamic for a better-managed church was coming from the outside and represented well-heeled Catholic donors. It had key players inside the Vatican like Cardinals Szoka and Castillo Lara, working with the support of Pope John Paul II. Yet, even with this powerful confluence of cooperators, the effort was of only limited impact.

By 2018, the former president of the Vatican Bank would stand trial with coconspirators for embezzling some sixty-two million dollars in connection with the sale of Vatican real estate properties over a seven-year period starting in 2001. While the IOR would experience a complete overhaul in leadership and its operations under the papacy of Pope Francis, sadly, chronic corruption continued to prove a formidable foe, thriving like a deadly bacterial culture in the darkness and secrecy that are allowed to typify so much of the church's handling of money.

This situation will probably not improve until those who provide the church with its funds insist upon more exacting standards of accountability and stewardship at all levels of its institutional ministry.

Unfortunately, many Catholics have a long way to go before such demands catch fire at the local level. Parish research finds typical Sunday Mass attendees in the United States almost completely uninformed about the actual use of the nearly eight billion dollars in yearly donations they make to the Catholic collection basket.

"Follow the money" became a popular and much-quoted phrase

in Washington's post-Watergate era, and now it has become a mantra in investigative journalism and political debates. Today, it is a quintessential principle in maintaining institutional integrity and trust. With the horrendous damage caused by the revelations of decades of clergy sexual abuse, the importance of account-ability is inarguable. It must be evident on every operational level of the church, including its use of the faith community's financial resources.

9

Aid in a Time of Solidarity

Cardinal Jozef Tomko, a Slovak running one of the most important funding agencies in the Holy See, the Congregation for the Evangelization of Peoples, was considered one of the more accessible and welcoming faces in Rome.

He was close to Pope John Paul II, whose papacy was playing a dramatic role in the liberation of Poland and the collapse of the Soviet Union.

FADICA's first visit to Rome began a friendship with Cardinal Tomko that we cultivated over the years so that, during our interactions with Cardinal Szoka in Rome, I would always also manage a call to Cardinal Tomko to say hello. He not only had his pulse on Vatican affairs, but his position put him in touch with the entire globe. Because he was always looking for donors to help poorer dioceses of the world, the cardinal valued being kept informed of FADICA's interests.

As the Berlin Wall came down and Eastern Europe gained the ability to revive public worship, members of the Raskob family were particularly interested in helping Catholicism rebuild in the former Iron Curtain countries. Research by Raskob family members found the church in the United States ill prepared for what would soon become a major area of church expansion. One of the family members, Charles Robinson, suggested that the U.S. bishops undertake a program of church-to-church aid. The Raskob Foundation wished to join other donors in FADICA to get things started.

The default reflex of the United States Catholic Conference was triggered instantly by Robinson's suggestion. All proposals that involved the raising of money met instant death at the threshold. American pastors generally did not welcome money appeals for outside charities because they viewed passing the basket a zero-sum game. In their eyes, an additional appeal for a cause, no matter its merits, meant less charity to benefit their parishes and dioceses.

Yet research in fundraising consistently found the opposite to be true. The more people were asked to give, the stronger a culture of generosity in the parish became. Giving begets more giving.

Robinson, frustrated over the USCC's lack of solidarity with the church in Eastern Europe, asked me to try opening up a conversation at the conference. But my efforts also hit the proverbial brick wall. When I suggested a national effort, the idea was put before the USCC's Committee on Social Development, chaired then by Los Angeles cardinal Roger Mahony. Mahony, well attuned to the sentiment of his pastors and running one of the U.S. church's biggest fundraising efforts for the new $200 million Los Angeles Cathedral, Our Lady of the Angels, wanted no part of what would surely turn out to be a tap on precious local wealth.

The USCC spokesman, Msgr. Bob Lynch, conveyed to me the unhappy news of Cardinal Mahony's firm decision not to move forward with the Raskob Foundation's suggestion.

Weeks later, FADICA's Vatican management studies project brought me to Rome. I called Cardinal Tomko to let him know that I was in the city. He invited me to lunch at his villa near the Propagation of the Faith College adjacent to the Vatican.

Aware of Cardinal Tomko's roots in Eastern Europe, I asked him, "Will you be funding many of those dioceses in that part of the world?" Cardinal Tomko said that the Propagation of the Faith's worldwide portfolio and limited funds would be insufficient for the great needs emerging to rebuild seminaries and convents and start massive catechetical work even in his own country, let alone so many other Eastern European nations.

"What is really needed," he said, "is a new effort entirely. With the Holy Father's interest, maybe that can happen."

I had to suppress the urge to stand up and high-five the cardinal. I knew at that moment that Cardinal Mahony's earlier thumbs-down action was not the last word. "My colleagues will be especially happy to hear that," I said reassuringly. I told Cardinal Tomko what had happened at the USCC weeks earlier, and while saying nothing, he shook his head and stared ahead, looking lost in thought.

Days after the lunch with Cardinal Tomko, the USCC president, Archbishop Daniel Pilarczyk of Cincinnati, happened to be making one of his twice-yearly visits to the Vatican. This was a formal process for all bishops' conference presidents. During these visits, bishops report on priorities and receive information on any pending matters.

The Holy See is like a small village, so when someone like a representative of a bishops' conference is in town, word spreads quickly across the various congregations and offices. The visiting American archbishop was invited to stop by Cardinal Tomko's offices located near the Piazza di Spangna in a posh tourist section of central Rome.

Pilarczyk, a scholarly Ohioan, who had risen within the leadership of the church in the United States under the influence of Cardinal Joseph Bernardin, his predecessor in Cincinnati, was surprised by Tomko's detailed questions about the USCC's recent decisions on international aid. Until that moment, Pilarczyk knew nothing about Cardinal Mahony's reportedly negative decision on the Raskob Foundation's proposed U.S. Catholic aid for Eastern and Central Europe and Russia.

He assured Tomko that, in any case, the question was not a closed one since, he said, USCC committees can't make decisions by themselves. He promised Tomko that he would look into the matter.

Within three weeks of my visit to Rome, the chief administrator of the USCC, Msgr. Lynch, was on the phone to me, inviting foundation support to send three teams of U.S. bishops on a fact-finding trip to the newly emerging areas under former Soviet rule. Lynch invited FADICA members to travel along with the bishops.

One team would be going to Russia, the Baltic countries, and

Ukraine; another to Poland, the Czech Republic, Slovakia, and Romania; and a third would travel to Serbia and Albania.

The teams were to meet with clergy and laypeople in the once-underground church and then identify rebuilding plans—for example, reestablishing parishes and schools and restoring seminaries and colleges.

Cardinal Tomko's intervention had a huge impact on the USCC's reversal of plans. It was one of the rare moments when I understood why a top-down model of governance in the church could occasionally be beneficial in reinforcing the global dimension of Catholicism.

The teams embarked in late August 1991. I traveled to Russia with Ukrainian bishop Basil Losten of Connecticut and Bishop Paul Baltakis of New York, a Franciscan émigré born in Lithuania and former prisoner of war held captive by the Nazis in a forced labor camp. Archbishop John L. May of St. Louis and USCC staffer John Carr were also part of our team.

Exploring church rebuilding after the dissolution of the Soviet Union in 1991, a Catholic delegation from the USCC gathers in Moscow. Right to left: Archbishop John May of St. Louis; Bishop Basil Losten of the Ukrainian Greek Catholic Church of Catholic Diocese of Stamford, Connecticut; Msgr. Robert Stern of the Catholic Near East Fund; John Carr, USCC secretary for justice and peace; and Frank Butler, FADICA president

It was a remarkable expedition. Our out-of-date *Aeroflot* aircraft landed in Lithuania from Moscow, where our delegation met up with Chicago's Cardinal Joseph Bernardin. He would be the star of the show during this stop. Chicago has the largest group of expatriate Lithuanians in the world.

Flower girls in folk costumes and a large contingent of Lithuanian bishops, priests, sisters, and local officials greeted us on a sparkling August morning. We were driven to Vilnius, a beautiful medieval town that was in the midst of a melancholic ceremony: the reburial of hundreds of political and religious prisoners who had perished in Siberia under ruthless Soviet regimes. Coffins awaiting their home burial sites were stacked in rows near one of the holiest shrines in Vilnius, the Church of the Gate. We stopped to pray and pause in silence at the deeply riveting scene. Instantly, we had a lesson in the great suffering, loss, and heroism that distinguished our hosts' church during decades of religious suppression.

Days of beautiful liturgies and banquets followed, with plenty of time to meet and listen to prisoners newly freed under Mikhail Gorbachev's perestroika initiative. This new world-changing policy had shrunk Russia's empire to its pre-Soviet boundaries.

Alfonsas Svarinskas, SJ, a seventy-year-old Jesuit, approached me during a welcome ceremony. He had spent twenty-one years imprisoned in the coldest region of Siberia, where temperatures can sometimes reach minus fifty degrees Fahrenheit.

With the aid of a translator, Fr. Alfonsas told me that, on his arrival in Siberia to serve a sentence of hard labor, he had been chained inside an unheated outhouse for a few hours each day of teeth-chattering misery. He broke into a smile as he looked at the distress on my face and said he was very happy now to hear that people in America cared about Lithuania and were there to help the church get back on its feet.

I felt humbled to be in the presence of this serene Jesuit, whose faith led to his triumphant return to his beloved country and who did not seem to harbor any harsh resentments, only a joy at being home. I quietly thanked him and, later that night, tearfully thanked God for the privilege of meeting such holy people.

After our stay in this gorgeous and extraordinary nation, the prospect of reviving diocesan and parish structures and Catholic social services, long forbidden there, took on personal dimensions for all of us on the visitation team. There was no question that financial help, and so much more, was needed from U.S. Catholics.

August 1991 arrival in Lithuania. Left to right: Cardinal Joseph Bernardin of Chicago, Cardinal Vincentas Sladkevicius of Kaunas, and FADICA president Frank Butler

The journey continued. Bishop Baltakis's brothers, native Lithuanians, chauffeured us in weather-beaten Ladas jam-packed with suitcases and our delegation. We missed the comforts of the United States—roadside restaurants and rest stops—as we traversed barren Soviet military highways through endless de-populated forests and flatlands toward our southern destinations.

We stopped frequently. The gas cans attached to our roof al-lowed vapor to blow into the car. As we exited the car to breathe in the country air, we joked about headlines in the States reading, "U.S. Bishops Mysteriously Perish in Car Explosion."

Occasionally, we would stop to eat our prepacked meals and marvel at the wide horizon of the Ukraine. It was like Texas with-out fences, a chilling memorial actually to dictator Joseph Stalin, who consolidated Ukrainian family-owned farms and executed those who lived on them.

Lviv, a Ukrainian destination, surprised us with its elegant old-world architecture and bustling population. We were all travel-weary and eager to settle in for the night after a warm welcome from local clergy.

The next day was a bright Sunday. The Byzantine Rite Catholic Church of the Ukraine had just taken back its beautiful Cathedral of St. George from the Russian Orthodox Church. The Orthodox were favored by communist rulers. Soviet leaders had allowed the church to use many confiscated Catholic properties.

Now in the age of glasnost, the Russian Orthodox no longer had the upper hand in Ukraine as its people regained their autonomy and freedom. Church properties were being taken back by force by their rightful owners, a first step in restoring the Catholic community.

We were not the only outsiders arriving in Lviv to lend a hand. We met a young and charismatic American of Ukrainian ancestry who seemed to have a strategic sense of what was needed to revive Catholicism there. His name was Borys Gudziak, a brilliant thirty-year-old with a newly minted Harvard PhD.

Gudziak, a frequent visitor to Lviv, was in the process of starting an organization called the Institute of Church History. Later it would become the Ukrainian Catholic University.

At this time, when the Soviet Empire was still in the process of being dissolved, Gudziak had managed to bring into the Ukraine forbidden religious materials, including Bibles, under the guise of providing study materials for his institute. At the time of our arrival, he was holding a series of lectures in a local stadium on Christian culture. Ostensibly, it was an academic exercise, but existentially, it was an exercise in proselytizing—risky business because of the network of Soviet informants still in place.

One afternoon, our U.S. team visited with local volunteers putting the finishing touches on Gudziak's cultural program, collating printed materials for distribution. It provided an eye-opening education about the Greek Rite Catholic Church of the Ukraine.

We met ordained priests of that rite who were stuffing envelopes beside their wives and children. A bit confused by this scene, I approached one of the priests who sported a conventional Roman collar. After introducing myself and the purpose of our visit, I said, "So, are you Greek Orthodox?"

Looking at me quizzically, he laughed and answered, "If you are a Catholic from America, you and I have the same pope. No, we are not Greek Orthodox, but Greek *Rite* Catholics, known more formally as the Ukrainian Greek Catholic Church."

During my Catholic seminary study I often wondered about the rule preventing priests from marrying. Until this encounter, I was unaware that some priests, those among the Greek rite, were an exception, and had, since the rite's beginnings in the fourth century, featured a married clergy. Today, the rite comprises some ten million Catholics, an impressive size given the history of having been severely persecuted, especially during the twentieth century.

Later that day, I could not stop thinking about what I had learned. If there were such massive priest shortages in the United States, why couldn't the pope allow this practice—married priests—for Latin rite Catholics?

Our stop in Lviv and the other countries of Eastern Europe convinced us of how much we in the West had to learn from our fellow Christians in this part of the world, and how much we had to reflect upon when it came to Christian witness and endurance. We returned to the States more eager than ever to build further bridges of friendship.

Some months later, Archbishop John May of St. Louis—a member of our travel team to Russia, the Baltics, and Ukraine, and a highly respected former president of the USCC—made an eloquent and successful case to the U.S. hierarchy for the establishment of the new program of Catholic aid for Eastern and Central Europe and Russia.

Archbishop May's passionate conviction, seasoned by the long inspiring journey, carried the day. A unanimous vote for a national campaign of church aid to Eastern and Central Europe and Russia followed May's riveting report on the visits of all three USCC teams.

Looking back over two decades and a quarter of a billion dollars in charitable aid generated by American Catholics for church rebuilding in that part of the world, one appreciates how powerful a personal presence can be in changing hearts and motivating people to do the right thing. Because of its global connection and structure, Catholicism continues to play an important role in bridging global divides, while knitting together networks of solidarity and friendship. Today's ongoing campaign for Eastern and Central Europe and Russia is a testament to that fact.

But more than this, the experience for me was as deepening as were my travels at the age of eighteen with fellow seminarians serving the people of San Miguel, Mexico. Working shoulder to shoulder with hardworking campesinos and sharing their lives ever so briefly made the word "catholic" take on its universal dimension. In a day when walls seem to have such attraction for many governments of this world, including our own, I am grateful that my own church transcends borders and connects me with humanity around the globe.

10

A Dark History Revealed

Ironically, the bishops' generosity and expressions of solidarity with retired religious and with the emerging church of Eastern and Central Europe did little to offset their plummeting public image in the wake of revelations in 2002 of clergy sexual abuse—an issue that would eventually lead to the brink of disaster for the Catholic Church in the United States and elsewhere.

The roots of the problem ran more deeply than most Catholics were aware. The individual tragedies were recorded in secret church archives while predatory clergy were shifted about by their bishops and allowed to continue to prey on young people.

Then one day, the problem came to light. Investigative reporting by Jason Berry, published in 1986 in the *National Catholic Reporter* involving the Reverend Gilbert Gauthe, a pedophile priest in the Diocese of Lafayette, Louisiana, triggered reports and promises by the Catholic hierarchy to take action.

Yet the issue disappeared from national consciousness until, sixteen years later in 2002, the *Boston Globe*'s Pulitzer Prize–winning investigative reporting drew the public's attention to the clergy abuse problem in the Archdiocese of Boston.

Cardinal Bernard Law's behavior in reassigning two molesting priests, the Revs. John Geoghan and Paul Shanley, managed to command not only Boston's attention but also that of an entire nation.

Four years prior to the *Globe*'s reporting, the Archdiocese of Boston had reportedly settled fifty civil suits with Geoghan's alleged victims for more than $10 million. Paul Shanley, with accusations tying him to abuse that went back years, had been quietly transferred by the Archdiocese of Boston to a diocese in California, where he carried out pastoral duties while local church officials were kept in the dark about his horrific past.

The *Globe* used both the Geoghan and Shanley cases to bring to light a much longer history of the Archdiocese of Boston's handling of child molestation claims against seventy of its priests. As a result of the *Globe*'s investigation, Cardinal Bernard Law found himself surrounded by enraged parishioners and victims' families wherever he made public appearances.

That same year, following the *Globe*'s expose, during the annual American Cardinals' Dinner—a benefit for the Catholic University of America held that year at a hotel in Philadelphia—the sudden descent in public esteem of Cardinal Law and that of his fellow bishops nationwide was unmistakably apparent.

Fran and I, both alums of CUA, were among the invited guests of FADICA's Tom Donnelly, who also served on the CUA board. During the reception just prior to the dinner, Fran and I were talking among other guests in the hushed atmosphere of the hotel's atrium. One prominent monsignor, a CUA trustee, assured the small group gathered around us that the "Cardinal Law business" would "all blow over soon."

Fran turned to the self-assured monsignor and replied unwaveringly: "No, Monsignor, this is not going to blow over." The stunned priest gently nodded and slid away, pretending to recognize another arriving guest. But the episode captured the great divide between the way laypeople and clergy were understanding the dimensions of the problem of priestly sexual abuse and diocesan cover-ups. One side was horrified by what had happened to children, and the other tended to see it as a bump in the road.

Normally, Cardinal Law and his counterparts would be seated with major donors and distinguished guests at this annual event. Law was the board chair of Catholic University. Yet those in attendance, including fellow members of the hierarchy, seemed to go to great lengths to dodge the cardinal, not wanting to be photographed with him.

A tsunami of media coverage followed Cardinal Law wherever he went. He quickly became a poster boy for the church's abuse crisis. The Philadelphia hotel was surrounded by satellite dish–laden trucks and camera crews whose numbers surpassed even the event's donor attendees.

The scope of the problem in Boston set off a long stream of media reporting across the nation, fueled in part by the historic meeting of American bishops a month later in Dallas. By then, the public had been exposed to what looked like a systematic policy of hiding widespread criminal abuse of children by priests and religious that included using church funds to silence and litigate against the complaining parents of abuse victims.

Lifelong Catholics, like those in our philanthropic network, were livid and demoralized. Their charity aimed to help an institution whose leaders had broken trust and dishonored Catholicism in an unprecedented way. The brand name "Catholic" seemed seriously tarnished by the *Globe*'s disclosures and by the endless stories of deceit and human injury that followed.

It was a low point for our work in FADICA. I was beginning to doubt that we could ever partner again with the bishops as we had in helping religious orders with their retirement or aiding church-rebuilding efforts in Eastern Europe. Clergy sexual abuse and its cover-up seemed a depressing if not fatal blow for what we were trying to do at FADICA: create a spirit of cooperative, church-oriented philanthropy.

I received a providential call from my older brother, Al, about this time, and it influenced me to think about FADICA's role in a completely different way.

Al, a newly retired General Electric executive, functioned as a wisdom figure, a mentor for me ever since our dad's untimely death during our youth. I welcomed hearing his voice on the phone one evening when the clergy abuse crisis led the national news headlines just after the U.S. bishops meeting in Dallas adopted an abuse prevention and reporting strategy for the nation's dioceses.

Al asked me whether the Dallas meeting was just a publicity stunt. The bishops had pledged themselves to the establishment of a national oversight board of independent laypeople who would monitor compliance by the church with a strict program of prevention and reporting on child abuse. It was referred to as a "zero tolerance" policy.

"Seems to me," Al suggested, "that your group of Catholic donors is in a position to influence the direction of things in a significant way."

"How is that?" I asked, bewildered and discouraged by the depth and breadth of the abuse crisis.

"Well," he continued, "someone ought to strengthen that commission of independent laypeople overseeing the plan adopted in Dallas before some powerful bishop tries to choke off its funding, or compromise its work."

There was too long a history of covering up clergy abuse, and Al was probably right: people don't change a system when they hold all the power. Eventually, any lay watchdog group was bound to bump heads with the bishops.

As the late summer approached, I received a call from attorney Robert Bennett, a prominent Washingtonian and one of the new members of the independent lay board looking into clergy sexual abuse. Our wives volunteered together in local charities, and we were also neighbors.

Bob asked for my help as he searched for candidates for the new child protection office at the USCCB (now known as the United States Conference of Catholic Bishops) where he served as a volunteer on the first lay board overseeing the bishops' abuse prevention program and the new child protection office. This office would also support the work of his independent lay oversight board. He stressed his preference for a candidate with a law enforcement background.

I did not think I could help him because I knew so few in the law enforcement field, but nevertheless I was happy to be asked and kept thinking about Bob's search in the days ahead.

One afternoon, I had a providentially timed lunch with a friend who did volunteer work with me. This chance meeting opened an important door that benefited Bennett's search.

Ed Reilly was a former Kansas legislator and, at the time of our lunch, a U.S. Parole Commission chair. He was raising a young son alone after the untimely passing of his wife, Luci. Ed's day job at the parole commission involved granting or denying parole for federal prisoners.

In the middle of our conversation about our volunteer work, Bob Bennett's request came to mind. Ed was not only surrounded by law enforcement professionals because of his work, but he was a devout Catholic and understood how important Bennett's new lay commission would be in preventing future crimes involving clergy sexual abuse of young people.

Ed Reilly was a gold mine of ideas. Instantly, he gave me the names of a Medal of Honor winner, a top state police commissioner, and an assistant director of the FBI. It was the last one who turned out to be the most promising. Kathleen McChesney had had a twenty-four-year career with the FBI, working her way up to become special agent in charge of the Chicago Division, assistant director of the Training Division, and eventually, the executive assistant director of the FBI for Law Enforcement Services.

Reilly called me some days following our lunch and reported that McChesney was about to retire from federal service and would be interested in knowing more about the new lay oversight board. I gleefully reported the news to Bob Bennett and shortly after that learned that an interview had been arranged.

The rest clicked into place. Kathleen was appointed as director of the new USCCB Office for Child Protection. Over the following months and years, Kathleen McChesney, working with Bennett's board, developed the first comprehensive screening and training program to combat child sex abuse in the Catholic Church. Catholic dioceses were now held to national standards and were annually audited for compliance.

While the new program of church oversight was being built, I continued to think about the financial dimensions of the scandal. Most Catholics were aghast at the amount of money involved in the settlements paid by the nation's dioceses. Were donations being diverted to pay such settlements or to hush-up complaints?

No one really knew because Catholic dioceses at that point were not required to file tax forms or publish independent audits that might supply such information. Reporters got their figures from court records where they could. Those records that were available indicated that lots of money expended for litigation was under the radar for the average Catholic.

It was time for me to talk with someone experienced in finding financial shenanigans in church operations.

Kathleen McKinless, a partner at one of the nation's biggest accounting firms and a forensic auditor experienced in church financial fraud, had impressed our FADICA foundations when she spoke before them on diocesan accounting practices years before the *Globe's* investigation of clergy abuse. Kathleen was one of the few people in the country who had extensive experience in unlocking the mysteries of church financial reports.

This experienced and insightful CPA worked only a few blocks from the FADICA offices in the Dupont Circle neighborhood of Washington, so I visited her one morning looking for ideas on how the Catholic bishops' new lay oversight program on clergy sexual abuse might use financial reporting as a tool to shed light on the diocesan practices.

Generally, dioceses were not required under Canon Law or civil law to publish their financial information, so, in most cases, Catholics had no idea about the millions of dollars passing through church institutions that allowed the abuse crisis to go undetected.

It was apparent from the start of our conversation that Kathleen McKinless was familiar with all kinds of nonprofit organization reporting. The tax-exempt sector was growing, and her audit practice included a wide range of nonprofits, including Catholic dioceses. Kathleen knew the diocesan culture and had been called in more than once to follow the trails of malfeasance occurring in dioceses.

She went right to work reviewing and reformulating drafted questions I'd brought with me, hoping to save time, which it did. The finished product of our conversation was ready within an hour. I learned in the process how dioceses sometimes hide their financial activities through separate corporations, masking their wealth and property holdings, or providing only partial information on their chancery—central administration—and its liabilities.

After a few edits, we both felt that the new accounting tool might work. We had a set of questions that would produce the expenditure numbers that would compel disclosure of the economic costs to dioceses linked to the clergy sexual abuse scandal. Now it was time to meet the new program director of the Office for Child Protection.

My image of an FBI agent was anything but the warm, friendly, and outgoing person who walked into the restaurant where I met Kathleen McChesney for lunch. "So how in the world do you know Ed Reilly?" Kathleen asked as she beamed and shook my hand.

Though Kathleen was new to the USCCB, as an experienced investigator she was way ahead in appreciating the financial underpinning of criminal behavior. Without my explaining FADICA's concerns as a donor organization, Kathleen immediately understood my motivation in wanting to meet her. "I'll bet the folks you work with want to know what role if any did donated money play in covering up clergy sexual abuses," she said, as we jumped right into an animated discussion.

"Gee," I responded, "you read my mind. This is going to be easier than I thought." I handed Kathleen the piece of paper and explained its suggested financial survey questions we had framed for Catholic dioceses.

She welcomed FADICA's input. The new program director made no firm promises but assured me that she would share the questions with the USCCB. I was struck by her candor and left with the impression that the new Office for Child Protection had managed to find an individual with an instinct for investigation and depth. I also wondered how long she would last as she and her commission ran into the roadblocks and diversions they were sure to encounter.

The financial survey questions were eventually given the green light by the USCCB. Over the next year, survey results were made public. At that time, about a billion dollars in litigation and settlements involving the sexual abuse of children by priests was now documented. The sum grew more steeply with the coming years. By the year 2015, that number increased fourfold. Nine archdioceses and dioceses filed for bankruptcy.

The reckless use of church donations to enable clergy offenders to continue their abuse over years, even decades, angered and perplexed Catholics in the pews. But it had a particularly grievous effect on foundations and donors who had structured much of their giving to help Catholic institutions.

FADICA's meetings were now focused exclusively on accountability and financial stewardship. Conversations seemed different. A signature affability that had marked our get-togethers now morphed into high wariness. Distrust of an unaccountable church management replaced a normally upbeat attitude toward working with the church.

A national survey by Gallup commissioned by FADICA about this time revealed that the majority of Mass-attending Catholics remained in the dark about where their donations actually went. Nearly 80 percent of Catholics wanted the bishops to provide a more fulsome accounting of the use of their donations.

Catholics who had been formed in a church of *pray, pay, and obey* were waking up to a nightmare, and they wanted more answers. Parish collections in the dioceses coping with abuse plummeted. Boston, where the archdiocesan annual fund brought in $17 million in the year 2000, experienced a tailspin in fundraising, reporting only $8.6 million after the *Boston Globe* revelations.

With the Boston scandal still on the front pages of American dailies, Francis Oakley and Bruce Russett at Yale University Law School brought together a cross-section of theologians, journalists, and executives for a conference in June 2002 titled Governance, Accountability, and the Future of the Catholic Church.

In a paper I delivered at this New Haven gathering, I noted that, amid the clamor over clergy sexual abuse, no concrete strategy had yet surfaced to bring about a more accountable church management.

Days later, Tom Reese, SJ, who was the editor of *America*

magazine and co-presenter at the Yale conference, called me on behalf of a fellow Jesuit, Donald Monan, SJ, chancellor of Boston College. Monan and a friend of his, a BC alumnus named Geoff Boisi, wanted to talk with me about their interest in the subject that I had just addressed.

I invited Fr. Monan and Geoff Boisi to speak at a FADICA board meeting planned in Memphis in the coming weeks. The two briefed the FADICA board about the abuse crisis in Boston and in Boisi's home diocese of Rockville Centre, New York. They revealed their own plans to allow business leaders to speak at an upcoming conference about needed improvements in church management. Boisi said that the governing committee of the USCCB was expected to attend.

In early July 2003, the conference opened at the John Paul II Cultural Center near the USCCB in northeast Washington, DC. Boisi invited dozens of luminaries from business and media and the Catholic world. I was invited as well to lead a postluncheon discussion on the communications aspect of the abuse crisis.

While the meeting began with good-natured remarks, it quickly degenerated into a heated shellacking for the bishops present. Both sides, lay and hierarchy, seemed to boil inside as the conference wore on.

The bishops were the proverbial fish in a barrel. The hard feelings about what seemed now to be more of an ambush rather than a dialogue lasted for weeks afterward. Boisi phoned me several times to express his consternation over the hierarchy's "thin skin" and disgust over the bishops' refusal to accept responsibility for the tragedy unfolding in the church in the United States.

Prospects for further dialogue looked improbable. Boisi was stumped. "It's ironic how available these guys are when they want to discuss donations," Boisi remarked. "But when you say anything critical, they scatter."

"Try to swallow your frustration," I advised Boisi. "Focus instead on constructive steps that are easy to take." Years at the USCCB and with FADICA had taught me that tilting at windmills within the church sometimes produces actual results—a fact due more to the underlying function of grace than our intentions or competence.

Confrontation seldom seemed to be as effective with Catholic bishops as offering something practical and helpful. We had learned this over a long period of time. A foundation's complaint, for instance, about poor financial reporting by Catholic dioceses was nowhere near as impactful as the decision to initiate and fund a remedial program to train church employees in the latest accounting standards.

I encouraged Boisi to try again with a discussion involving business leaders and bishops. This time, I said, locate it in a business setting. The Wharton Business School, where Boisi served as a board member, would be ideal, I told him. If Boisi recast the project as a work of cooperation to strengthen church management systems, it just might communicate a more sympathetic objective and practical benefit.

By mid-summer of 2004, two years after the *Boston Globe* reports, Geoff Boisi presided over a revised version of his hoped-for dialogue. This time, the location was one of the most prestigious business schools in the nation: Wharton, at the University of Pennsylvania.

Two hundred people, comprising Catholic organizational leaders and business CEOs, were present. Boisi landed the archbishop of San Francisco, William Levada, a rising star in Rome, as the opening speaker. Levada had just cleaned up a nasty financial mess in Santa Rosa, California. It was a diocese rife with sexual scandal and financial chicanery. The archbishop had seen firsthand what can happen when management controls in a diocese are weak. He was passionately committed to strengthening administrative structures for dioceses.

The gathering in the state-of-the-art $139 million Huntsman Hall of Wharton in downtown Philadelphia consisted of breakout discussions on church accountability and management practices. Boisi spent nearly a quarter of a million dollars on exceptional logistics for the get-together, sending a message to church leaders that he was deadly serious about this undertaking. Arrangements included professional teams of conference organizers, discussion facilitators, and speakers who gave laser focus to the two-day meeting.

Boisi wanted things to move beyond the criticisms to practical action. He announced the formation of an entirely new organization capable of resourcing management ideas and standards for U.S. Catholic dioceses.

A former work colleague of Boisi's from his Goldman Sachs days, Thomas Healey, a Wharton attendee and a FADICA board member, volunteered to help Boisi with his plan. Just days after the meeting, Healey produced a crisply worded report containing thirty-seven management reforms that conference participants had endorsed. The report called for fundamental changes in how church funds were handled, compliance with national accounting standards, better planning and oversight, and ongoing performance reviews of church employees.

All measures were practical and feasible except one. It dealt with the appointment of bishops. For decades, the church had followed a secret process where loyalty and orthodoxy in bishop candidates played more of a decisive role than management ability. But the Wharton conference resolution, while recognizing the Holy See's preeminent role in the appointment of bishops, called for improvements in "the existing process for selecting bishops (by) including a clear definition of qualifications (including managerial capabilities), face-to-face interviews, and well-informed nominations and recommendations from clergy and laity."

The Boisi team was stepping on the third rail of both the Vatican and provincial archbishops in the United States—those exclusively in charge of the most important decision about church governance: the choice of leaders. It was a resolution that seemed to me on target but politically a nonstarter. I questioned whether it would threaten the entire Boisi church management project.

"That's precisely the problem," argued Boisi by phone one day following the Wharton meeting. "No one is willing to talk about the way bishops are chosen, and that is the elephant in the room." Boisi was connected by conference call with colleague Tom Healey,

Fr. Monan, and me. Boisi was right. And looking back following the scandals involving the promotions of corrupt cardinals and bishops revealed years later, the Wharton resolution today takes on prophetic dimensions.

Yet, aware of the failure of the first attempt by Boisi to dialogue with leading bishops, I told the threesome that they seemed to be skating on thin ice.

The Wharton resolutions and report were published. Soon thereafter, a previously issued invitation to Boisi to address the diocesan financial officers of the United States was suddenly and mysteriously withdrawn. Was this the result of the controversial resolution on the selection of the bishops' process? No one seemed to know for sure, but doors to the bishops started to close.

The bishop of Gary, Indiana, Dale Melczek, who had attended the Wharton meeting, was a welcomed exception. Melczek, a saintly and wise leader, intuited the positive intent of Boisi's actions. He viewed as a good thing Boisi's sincere and generous effort to help the church restore trust and move its institutions and leadership into greater accountability. In his view, the resolutions of Wharton were deserving of consideration.

Melczek, a neighbor of Cardinal Francis George of Chicago, who had just been elected president of the USCCB, arranged an appointment for Boisi to clarify his intentions personally with the most influential member of the U.S. bishops.

The cardinal received Boisi, Fr. Monan, and a new staff director for Boisi's project, Kerry Robinson (Peter Robinson's gifted and dynamic daughter), at his archdiocesan offices on a cold fall day. I was asked to accompany the delegation as well and now served on the project's new board.

Cardinal George shook hands quickly with those present and took his seat to signal that he wanted to cut any small talk and get on with his day. "I am familiar with this project, Mr. Boisi," the cardinal said with a tense, unsmiling face, preempting any time-consuming explanations "and also with the meeting in Washington with the executive committee of the USCCB."

That reference alerted us that Cardinal George was about to give us a lecture.

"Frankly, members of the USCCB wonder what your objective is," the cardinal said as his eyes locked onto Boisi's.

Boisi gently interrupted George and made a much-repeated speech about the abuse crisis, diminished trust of laypeople, and the willingness of individuals in the business world to help church leaders manage better.

"Who asked for this help?" the cardinal asked, not really expecting an answer.

A period of awkward silence followed. I decided to jump in, as anger seemed not far from surfacing. "Baptized Catholics don't need an invitation," I piped up. "At least that's what I was taught when someone explained why we were obligated to contribute to the support of our church. Aren't we equally responsible for the life of the church?"

The cardinal just stared at me, and then, while avoiding a direct answer to my question, said, "Look, I am responsible for this archdiocese. Everything is held in my name as the archbishop. I do not have to ask you or anyone to tell me what I need to do. In fact, I've got plenty of advisory boards and professionals handling all that."

"With all due respect, Cardinal," Boisi objected, "we are not doing that. We invited the bishops to come to Wharton to talk with good people with deep business backgrounds about what's needed to rebuild trust in the management of the church. Sadly, we didn't get much of a response to our invitation from your brother bishops," Boisi added.

The cardinal scribbled a few notes to himself. His mood seemed to have improved after Boisi's firm rejoinder. The cardinal began to talk more as a coach and less as a commander, suggesting that Boisi and his colleagues would find their efforts more welcomed if public criticisms of the hierarchy were toned down and practical help to individual dioceses were offered.

"Time to say less and do more," the cardinal advised.

While Boisi was not eager to raise funds for dioceses, he saw the wisdom in Cardinal George's advice as an opportunity to show the benefits of good management practices. We left the meeting grateful for the frank exchange and the chance to dispel the misperceptions about Boisi's project, known as the National

Leadership Roundtable on Church Management (later shortened to Leadership Roundtable).

Shortly thereafter, an opportunity to show the benefits of good management practices presented itself. Weeks prior to the Chicago meeting, one of the deadliest hurricanes to hit the United States roared ashore in the Gulf of Mexico, flattening and flooding many cities in the southern states, and especially New Orleans.

In late August 2005, Hurricane Katrina displaced hundreds of thousands of people as swollen streams breached levies and flooded the city of New Orleans. Eighty percent of the city remained submerged for weeks while some fourteen hundred of its residents perished. Whole institutions were wiped out—schools and colleges, nursing facilities, and hospitals were massively damaged.

The Catholic Church, a historic, foundational presence in the New Orleans community, was left in terrible shape. An incredible array of seemingly insurmountable challenges faced New Orleans' Archbishop Alfred C. Hughes. This Philadelphia native seemed undeterred by what faced him and his surrounding community. He led efforts strategically important to putting the entire city of New Orleans back on its feet. Key among them was the use of Catholic schools.

Archbishop Hughes took lessons from the Hurricane Andrew recovery in Florida in 1992 that set record recovery time by returning children to their school classrooms. Knowing that opening the flooded public schools would take huge effort and therefore command a longer start-up time, Hughes generously opened up his parochial schools to *all* New Orleans children.

Following Boisi's Chicago sit-down with Cardinal George, I suggested to him that his new National Leadership Roundtable on Church Management had an unprecedented moment to act on George's advice: *Do more and say less.*

Boisi flew to New Orleans and began a conversation with Archbishop Hughes. Within weeks, Boisi had linked the Archdiocese of New Orleans to the McKinsey & Company management consulting firm and one of its brainiest and talented partners, Geno Fernandez, a former seminarian and Rhodes scholar.

Geno would spend the next several months based in the Archdiocese of New Orleans, completely reconfiguring the entire archdiocesan school system of some forty thousand students in order to accommodate the additional public school enrollments due to Katrina. In addition, Fernandez provided the archbishop with a succinct method of monitoring and measuring performance in his Catholic schools. This would turn out to be an enormously impactful management tool in future school planning.

As the New Orleans recovery progressed, word spread across the country of the Roundtable's help. More bishops and diocesan representatives began to show up at roundtable events. Cardinal George's advice was working.

Geoff Boisi's persistence and tangible help to a widening network of dioceses resulted in a vindication of his original intuition that the state of management in the church drove larger problems like that of clergy sexual abuse. The Roundtable would go on to find fewer skeptics and more influence in the nation's dioceses. Its standards and consultant services have introduced a best-practice culture in a growing number of diocesan and parish operations, saving millions of dollars in church expenses while improving the performance and accountability of church workers, both lay and clergy.

Perhaps the best aspect of Boisi's initiative was the blow it struck at the wall between clergy and laity—two completely separate worlds and cultures—a wall that accounts for so many of the church's problems.

The lesson learned both for church leaders and lay faithful in the start-up of the National Leadership Roundtable on Church Management is that an accountable and competently managed church won't come about on its own. Laypeople must demand improvement and higher standards of accountability, and they must persist in pushing back against the structural resistance to change. The success of the church in fulfilling its mission depends on it.

11

Catholic Schools in America

It is true that the Catholic Church's clergy sexual abuse crisis opened many eyes to the poor state of church management. But six decades of parochial school closings should have given more than a hint that church leadership was failing to cope with its basic responsibilities.

I often thought about my years with Catholic philanthropists and how much their generosity and interest in the church was attributable to the powerful influence of their parochial school formation.

My journey from parochial school, to the seminary, to a church-related career, to the importance I attached to a spouse who shared my faith, reflected in many ways the priceless religious formation of my Blessed Sacrament, St. Rita's, and Our Lady of Lourdes schools. There was a reason my years in those places provided many of my happiest childhood memories. Those institutions anchored me to the Christian community forever and even now, amid the tempest of church scandals and polarized divisions, they keep me focused on the Christian message of loving one's neighbor and looking out for the poor.

My personal experience in those Catholic schools leads me to believe that future generations of the faithful will look critically on church leaders of this era who allowed these schools to decline so precipitously—from five million students in the 1960s to slightly more than a million and a half students in 2020.

Catholic schools have been the engine room for the church: dynamos producing its clergy, its donors, its volunteers, and its more active parishioners. Research shows that Catholic school students are more likely to pray daily, attend church more often, retain their Catholic identity as adults, and donate more to the church than their counterparts in Catholicism who did not benefit from a parochial school education.

Waves of immigration in recent decades have swelled the ranks of U.S. Catholics, yet ironically, Catholic schools continue to close for want of students. In a time when Hispanic Catholics in the United States now comprise over half of the Catholic population under age thirty, fewer than 5 percent of their children are enrolled in Catholic schools. Most are deterred from attending by existing high tuition costs or the absence of Catholic schools close to them.

What will this mean over time in terms of institutional allegiances, worldview, and formal knowledge and practice of the faith for many of these younger Catholics? The very institutions that were created to accommodate the great waves of immigration of the late nineteenth century are now out of reach for most young Catholics of our day.

Immigration prompted the Catholic hierarchy over a century ago to mandate the establishment of a Catholic school in every parish of the United States. This was among the U.S. bishops' most consequential decisions. It enriched American Catholicism with religious vocations and contributed to the upward mobility of generations of Catholics, while shaping their thinking and behavior as a Christian community.

The impressive century-long upward rise of American Catholics can be seen as a product of an educational grounding provided by a massive network of accessible parochial schools, staffed by hundreds of thousands of religious women and men whose free labor made possible a quality education.

As this grand aspect of Catholicism now fades, the subject of parochial schools seldom commands the attention it deserves. Not one of the twelve national parish appeals sponsored by the Catholic bishops today aims to benefit Catholic schools, despite the capacity of parish collections to generate millions of dollars in support of global and domestic missions, antipoverty work, and even the U.S. bishops' Catholic University of America.

Would this be the case if church leaders and Catholics in the pews truly understood the long-term impact of parochial school closures? What are the reasons for this half-century of decline and neglect?

As religious women disappeared from Catholic classrooms in the 1960s and '70s, when their numbers declined due to aging, nearly all religious were replaced by lay teachers. This necessitated teacher salaries in a school system that previously had relied on free or low-salary work of teachers from religious orders. In addition, decades of Catholic social mobility out of America's urban centers and into geographic territory previously not served by Catholic schools necessitated that Catholic families seek their educational resources in the public system. Over time, the increased inability of existing parochial schools to compete for students and to pay for teaching talent created huge challenges. Many Catholic schools could not cope in a more competitive market. Church leadership appeared oblivious to what was happening.

From the perspective of Catholic philanthropy, a drastically smaller Catholic school sector appeared inevitable due to a lack of leadership and imagination. I learned in my years of working with private foundations that parochial school survival depended on exceptionally high-quality performance and model innovation. An entrepreneurial spirit of experimentation and improvement, driven by greater practices of accountability and measurement, were necessary components of any school that wanted to thrive.

We found such schools. They all were adopting new approaches. Many of them were willing to reach out to traditionally under-served populations. Just as for the first Catholic schools of decades before, lack of money was not allowed to be an excuse for turning away applicants for whom tuition was a factor.

One such example was a new model of a Catholic high school pioneered by the Jesuits. Its founder, Fr. John Foley, SJ, took part in one of FADICA's discussions about the future of Catholic schools in 1997, just after opening the school upon his return from missionary work in Latin America.

Foley had begun a work-study model of education for students from poor families patterned after a school in Lima, Peru. His Jesuit provincial suggested that he try to adapt the Peruvian model to a Chicago neighborhood called Pilsen/Little Village, an area with high concentrations of first-generation Latinos. He called the school Cristo Rey, which is Spanish for "Christ the King."

Students worked their way through high school in part-time jobs arranged through Cristo Rey. This eliminated the chronic financial problems typical Catholic schools encounter when they try to serve large numbers of families in lower income brackets. Chicago businesses served as partners for Cristo Rey by providing temporary employment for its students. Student compensation was paid directly to Cristo Rey and then applied to tuition costs. This enabled Cristo Rey students to take pride in paying their own way through school.

Under Father Foley's sunny and positive leadership, this new Jesuit venture at Cristo Rey took flight. It was rapidly duplicated in other states. Today there are nearly forty Cristo Rey high schools in the United States educating thousands of students from lower-income families.

B. J. Cassin, a Silicon Valley tech investor, provided much of the start-up capital needed to replicate Fr. Foley's model. Cassin brought his background in venture capital to enlist local sponsoring groups of donors. In the process, he became a godfather for this educational innovation. B. J., an alumnus of Holy Cross College, former Marine, and jazz aficionado, found that many Catholic fellow donors were enthusiastic about becoming partners with him in this new approach.

It was a watershed moment for those of us who had been watching the unchecked decline of Catholic schools. Now suddenly we were part of new high-quality Catholic educational startups that were flourishing. Their first-generation immigrant graduates entered the finest U.S. universities.

The Cristo Rey movement, while small in comparison with the overall twelve hundred secondary Catholic schools in America, was nonetheless demonstrating how laypeople, in formal partnership with religious orders, dioceses, and local businesses, could not only put together successful innovative versions of Catholic schools serving the poor, but also inspire and break through the fatalistic attitude present in too many diocesan chanceries and rectories about the future of Catholic schools.

The Cristo Rey successes held lessons for Catholic educators too, especially in promoting technology-based classrooms and a better system of measuring educational quality and teaching strength, while anchoring the school to a wider base of community support beyond Catholic circles.

This spirit of innovation explains another major Catholic school breakthrough. The University of Notre Dame's Alliance for Catholic Education (ACE) is an example of an initiative that injected new life into Catholic schools in underserved areas of the country by addressing the need for well-prepared teachers.

Ironically, Notre Dame had allowed its Graduate Department of Education to shutter its doors in 1977 amid an overall university realignment. Decades later, a growing concern over the state of K–12 education nationwide and a desire to encourage more postgraduate volunteer service among its students set the stage for a major reentry of Notre Dame into the field of education. The agent of change was a university political science professor, Fr. Timothy Scully, CSC.

Fr. Scully stopped by my office in Washington, DC, during his search for donors to help him get started with ACE. He was able to fund a good part of the program through the Corporation for National Service (CNS), a federal agency that funded teacher volunteer programs for underserved populations. Participation in the federal government's volunteer initiative meant that ACE teachers would not only qualify for a stipend but later they could receive financial help for graduate education. Because aspects of the ACE program involved faith formation, Notre Dame also needed private funds to supplement any federal grant they were to receive.

I was captivated by Scully's idea; his enthusiasm was contagious. After sharing some practical advice on which Catholic foundations to approach, I even asked Fr. Scully if my own daughter, Ellen, just graduating from Georgetown University, might apply.

Fr. Scully interviewed her the following day. Shortly thereafter, Ellen was invited to join forty graduates of Notre Dame in the first ACE class. Months later, I would visit Ellen and eight other remarkable ACE teachers who lived together in the Diocese of Lake Charles, Louisiana. The experience proved to be deeply formative for these teacher volunteers. It was also a godsend to a rural community challenged by a lack of teachers.

ACE in 2019 boasted almost two thousand graduates who served approximately 120 Catholic schools in sixteen states and thirty-one dioceses with serious shortages of clergy and religious. ACE has reached 180,000 students over its nearly twenty-five-year history.

In addition to their jump-starting the Cristo Rey high school movement, the Jesuits also have pioneered new educational approaches at the junior high or middle school level of education. Aimed to serve lower-income families, extended-day sixth-, seventh-, and eighth-grade schools began to spring up over the past two decades in many larger American cities. The Washington Jesuit Academy created in the early 2000s in the nation's capital is only one of them. It is a model of education that provides social, nutritional, and health services to nearly one hundred students in grades six, seven, and eight. Each student receives focused individualized attention from early morning until early evening, in an extended-year model of preparatory education. The school is run by an independent board and relies upon an impressive network of local donors and volunteers who value its groundbreaking approach and considerable social impact.

Still other inventive approaches in Catholic education include Boston College's City Connects, a revolutionary way of addressing the nonacademic barriers to learning that many lower-income students face. BC's program, developed by educational psychology professor Dr. Mary Walsh, brings a full range of the medical and social services available in surrounding communities into the Catholic urban schools in four states. Consequently, students have made remarkable strides in accessing services such as dental and medical care, counseling, and other basic needs right in their schools. The approach has been highly effective in reducing student attrition and improving overall student achievement.

Although some may consider Catholic schools a quaint left-over of a more protected Catholic culture of our immigrant past, these schools are more relevant to Catholicism's impact, internal strength, and forward progress than many clergy leaders seem to appreciate. The vitality of Catholic life and the church's contribution to the common good of society depends greatly on the quality, innovation, and competitive spirit of church-related schools.

In a church that desperately needs to rebuild trust and break down barriers after decades of clerical mismanagement and abuse, I can imagine few measures more necessary or timely than reviving Catholic education for a new era of shared responsibility and accountability.

12

A Deepening Faith

While Catholic schools have an outsized capacity to shape the Catholic spirit, so too has the vast array of Catholic spiritual traditions of prayer and reflection. I recognized this as I traveled throughout my life but especially with FADICA's members to destinations holding deep spiritual significance: Rome, the Holy Land, Ireland, and religious sites in this country as well.

Salient among these experiences was a trip to Israel intended as a visit with local Christian communities there to assess grant support for charitable works. A pilgrimage to the holy sites was also planned.

Nothing prepared me for the astounding beauty of today's Israel, with its lush farms and beautiful seacoast. The breathtaking scenes of where Jesus preached and ministered left impressions on me like no other geography.

On a gleaming midweek afternoon in 1996, thirty of us, mostly Catholic donors, quietly drifted on a large wooden tourist boat—a replica of St. Peter's fishing boat—on the Sea of Galilee, a freshwater lake about thirteen miles long and seven miles wide, known in some Gospel accounts as the place where Jesus called his first apostles to discipleship.

We read from Scripture, took in the site of the Mount of Beatitudes in the distance, and let our imaginations guide us back through the ages. The glassy stillness and bright sun lit up the gorgeous geography of this sacred area where the historical Jesus once walked. This group experience forever enriched the way I would hear the Scriptures read at Mass and picture the settings of the stories of the Gospels. Seeing a place for yourself and sensing all aspects of it allows you to know something in a vivid, more complete way. This is especially true in a spiritual context.

It was for this reason, too, that our gathering for Mass in the Church of the Holy Sepulcher in Jerusalem was so profound. This church is ground zero for Christians of the world. It is built over the sacred sites of the death and resurrection of Jesus.

Monsignor Robert Stern, then-director for the Catholic Near East Welfare Fund, who toured with us, made it possible for us to join him for Mass only a short distance from the tomb of Jesus. The spiritual and psychological impact of worship and prayer so close to the site of the Resurrection was unlike any spiritual exercise any of us could remember. It seems that our minds are not designed to absorb such powerful surroundings. Despite my best efforts to take in the reality that we were gathered near the spot of the encountered risen Lord, it felt dreamlike—far removed from the nettlesome ecclesiastical and institutional needs that occupied so much of my attention when it came to the subject of Catholicism.

Shortly afterward, each of us queued at the shrine built over the tomb of Jesus known as the Edicule. Fran and I entered the small room built over the slab of stone that recent scientific work confirms is the place where Jesus's body was laid to rest.

A Coptic monk sat quietly aside the stone as small candles burned around the holy site. Fran and I knelt and prayed together and placed our hands on the stone. Awe and deep emotion overcame us. Scenes of the world's troubles and endless wars over the centuries coursed through my imagination, and my own history with its memories of loss and disappointment rose to the surface. I recalled the words of a sister in Our Lady of Lourdes School during Holy Week uttering sadly and quietly to our class, "Let us join our pain and sorrow to that of Christ's," and felt as though I had been here long before this moment thanks to the Catholic imagination instilled in me from my youth.

Here both of us knelt, wordless, in the holiest of surroundings.

The moment moved us more than any great preaching could. We exited with extraordinary feelings of wonder and reverence, and yes, tears. No wonder so many Christians have risked the perilous pilgrim journey to Jerusalem over the ages. The visit to the Holy Land was the jewel in the crown of places holding spiritual surprises for me. But several visits to Rome also broadened my understanding and deepened my spiritual sensibilities through exposure to the remnants of early Christianity in that ancient city.

In visiting the Vatican on a regular basis, I would sometimes arrange to tour excavations of ancient Rome. These experiences inevitably touched something deep within me. They also helped me appreciate the stark contrast between the simplicity of the early church and the imperious Catholic governance structure we now know. For example, the first gatherings of Christians in Rome were in homes rather than in basilicas and churches.

Nowhere was home-based worship contrasted with churches more visible than in the Basilica of St. Clement, near the Lateran Palace, the fourth-century residence of popes before the Vatican became the church's central location in Rome.

Here in those early days, a congregation of worshiping Christians comprised several families without a single dominant ruling officer. Christians would meet in homes to pray, share responsibility, and distribute tasks. They were loosely networked with other such family groups throughout the city. Later, after Constantine granted the church a favorable status in the fourth century, the church took on a governmental structure similar to that of the Roman Empire. It became ruled by bishops and organized in units resembling today's dioceses.

The present-day St. Clement's church was built in the twelfth century. Touring the archaeological digs below this basilica, as FADICA members did following Mass there, I remember climbing down to the vestiges of a first-century home of a Roman nobleman and the place of Christian worship for a few families. Followers of Jesus gathered for a community meal there long before the building took on the contours of a church. I found the home aspect of Catholicism a wonderfully humble characteristic of the faith that now seems lost in its current officious structure.

The continuity of place unveiled in the layers of archaeological discoveries within St. Clement's offered a direct connection between the ancient age of fellow believers and our own. It made me appreciate the long history of my faith and the hardships and sufferings that fellow Christians endured for Christ and for the ages of Christians to come. *What blessings had they celebrated together?* I wondered. Were these early believers the ones who prompted the observation, "See how these Christians love one another?" The long perspective of time collapsed in the concentric circles of archaeological excavation of a hundred feet of earth, reminding me that the period of time that we occupy on this earth is indeed brief. How will our own Christian witness shape our age and those that follow?

Another of my favorite ancient sites in Rome is the tomb of St. Peter just below the grand basilica named after him. On more than one occasion I sought out this small chapel. It was a frequent site for the celebration of Mass with colleagues during our visits to the Vatican.

The location is only yards from what was the ancient Circus of Nero, an execution site during the era of Christian persecution. The small chapel is located under what was once the first basilica of St. Peter's, erected in AD 320, not long after Emperor Constantine's conversion.

The small reliquary in the chapel contains the remains of the first Apostle and serves as another link to the ancient roots of Catholicism. This tiny, cavelike chapel, dwarfed by the gigantic St. Peter's above it, was another apt contrast between the simplicity and humility of early Christianity and today's triumphant church structure, towering above it and shouting in so many ways, "power and wealth!" A drama within Catholicism over time has been between forces luring its adherents toward worldly concepts of achievement and that of its founder, who linked his church inextricably to the poor and lowly of the earth.

If one seeks an additional place in Italy that echoes the founding spirit of Catholicism, one travels only hours from Rome. The town of Assisi and the tomb of St. Francis contain the aura of this great saint, known for his love of simplicity and his joy of serving the poor.

Assisi was our destination on the occasion of the millennial celebration for the year 2000, when FADICA held a symposium there. Following lectures in a small hotel aside a mountain overlooking nearby farms, Fran and I enjoyed a leisurely stroll through the town. We then toured the famous Basilica of St. Francis. The main church is also on a hill that provides a panoramic view of the verdant countryside of Umbria. The tomb of St. Francis is in the church's crypt, providing visitors with a simple and tranquil place to pray, which we did together—leaving us with a sense of peace and joy.

St. Francis called the church back to its roots in poverty and showed a selfless love for neighbor in acts of mercy and kindness. This great legacy of St. Francis not only renewed the church of his time but continues to impact our era through brother Franciscans. The principal teachings and life story of this great saint have even shaped the papacy of the present pope, who summed up Francis of Assisi this way: "For me, Francis is the man of poverty, the man of peace, the man who loves and protects creation. . . . He is the man who gives us this spirit of peace, the poor man . . . and how I would like a Church which is poor and for the poor!" ("Address to Representatives of the Communications Media," March 16, 2013).

The opportunities to visit the historical settings of those who lived the faith in inspiring ways expanded my appreciation for the interplay of the Catholic faith over the ages with the cultures in which the faith took form. This is especially true of my own ancestral roots among the Irish people.

I took FADICA members to Northern Ireland in the years just after the peace accords were signed in 1998. We had a rare opportunity to visit with members of the newly elected parliament and to visit with faith communities working for peace in Belfast. We also took advantage of the visit to learn something about early Christianity on the island.

Ireland's rugged but gorgeous landscape provided an unforgettable setting to appreciate an Irish understanding of place, the nexus of the physical and the spiritual worlds. We realized the importance in the Irish tradition of the natural environment and the surroundings of one's life. They are essentially channels to the divine as well as to the identity of one's self. These features of the Irish outlook predate Christianity, finding roots in the Celtic view that the divine presence was recognizable in the workings of nature. This view of the world allowed the Irish to be quite receptive to the sacramental connection of the created order with the spiritual in the teachings of early Christian missionaries.

Among our stops during the visit was the Glendalough Abbey, an eighth-century monastic settlement, a short drive from Dublin, where we took part in a conference on early Irish Christianity.

In the beautiful ruins of the abbey we gained an appreciation for the long history of the Catholic faith in that one place, dating back to just a few short centuries after the time of Christ.

As I took in the gorgeous countryside of Glendalough, I thought about my Irish ancestors whose lineage paralleled the lives of the monks who inhabited Glendalough for centuries upon centuries. I marveled at this sense of time and how hundreds of monastic settlements like this, nestled among the lakes and mountains of Ireland, nourished and protected the faith and even the civilization that was passed along to me. How blessed I felt to be connected to the mystery and beauty of all this.

In addition to this exposure to Catholicism's rich cultural diversity through global travel, my colleagues in FADICA also found that the time set aside each year to reflect and to pray together exposed us to an incredible array of spiritualities in our faith tradition that we had known previously in name only.

In retreats each year, we interacted with a whole gamut of experts in the spiritual life. For example, we travelled to the Abbey of Gethsemani near Bardstown, Kentucky, to visit the tomb of one of the greatest spiritual writers of the twentieth century, Trappist Father Thomas Merton. While the monastic community there warmly hosted us, author Lawrence Cunningham, an expert on

Merton, walked us through this famous monk's spiritual journey.

Merton believed that, for the most part, Christianity had lost an appreciation for its mystical tradition. He had a deep understanding of what it was that people sought and experienced in their religious pursuits. It was far more than the neatly articulated dogmas and abstractions that often preoccupy church leaders. Merton offered fellow Christians his exploration of the deeper world of Christian mysticism and how to navigate the day-to-day struggle to discover the God who loves all of us. Merton's insights have influenced much in Catholicism since his death in 1968, especially interfaith conversation and social activism. Pope Francis, in his address before the U.S. Congress in 2015, praised Merton for opening new horizons for souls and for being a man of dialogue, a tool desperately needed in a world increasingly plagued by implacable divisions.

Spiritual writer Henri Nouwen was deeply influenced by Merton's work. We were privileged to have Fr. Nouwen lead us in a retreat outside Santa Barbara, California, shortly before his untimely death in 1996. He had been ministering at the time of our retreat at L'Arche Daybreak near Toronto, Canada, a community of people with developmental challenges. Nouwen wrote nearly forty books on the spiritual life, particularly aimed at reaching ordinary people with the message of acceptance and forgiveness found in the Christian Gospels.

A core aim of Nouwen's was to help others recognize God's dwelling within them. It was a remarkable experience to spend time with this spiritual teacher and encouraging fellow Christian, someone whose interests bridged the worlds of psychology and spirituality and whose powerful insights into the Christian message emerged from his own lifelong struggles with depression and loneliness.

The late Howard Gray, SJ, a theologian who taught for many years at several Jesuit universities, including Georgetown, proved to be a stellar guide to Ignatian spirituality—an approach to prayer and living that brings together the worlds of lived experience and faith.

Fr. Gray once led a gathering in California with my Catholic donor colleagues to familiarize us with the founder of the Jesuits, Ignatius of Loyola. This sixteenth-century saint, whose *Spiritual Exercises* have influenced millions of Catholics around the world through the community—the Society of Jesus—that he founded, pioneered a process of discernment that has helped people through the centuries make the connection between the experiences of daily living and understanding God's unique plan for each of us.

Fr. Gray's amiable personality, humor, and spiritual depth left us hungry to read and know more about St. Ignatius. A few years after this event, Fr. Gray arrived in Washington to teach at Georgetown. This, in turn, allowed me to ask Fr. Gray to direct me in the *Spiritual Exercises*. This yearlong experience revolutionized the way that I pray and helped me grow in awareness of God's companionship and loving presence.

Other extraordinarily accomplished spiritual writers who visited with our Catholic foundation community included Trappist Fathers Basil Pennington and Thomas Keating, who introduced us to centering prayer methods; British writer Rosemary Houghton, who helped us appreciate the graces of self-transformation at work within the Christian community; the brilliant Fr. Michael Himes of Boston College, whose use of humor and easy conversational style expanded our understanding of Christian leadership as service; and Fr. James Martin, SJ, a best-selling Catholic author and editor, who met with us in the beautiful high-country desert of Santa Fe to discuss the components of a saintly life.

Each of these experiences were outstanding and full of impact, demonstrating the spectacularly wide array of spiritual paths available to today's Christian. They were reminders of the importance of sacred space in the spiritual life, our connection with past generations of the faith community, and the astounding talent and goodness that continue to bless Catholicism in each age.

Today, the rediscovery of biblical spirituality and the spiritual classics, as well as the explosion of interest in prayer groups, Bible study, faith-inspired service and advocacy, meditation, and the urge to live a spiritually grounded life, are current trends inspiring Catholic spirituality. Catholics seem increasingly desirous of a church more deeply rooted in the faith it professes and more explicit about how each member of the church can discover and appreciate his or her own divine calling.

As I listened, reflected, and prayed in these various places with my faith community, I have been able to reap the benefits of praying more and worrying less, striving always to find God who meets me in the circumstances, blessings, and even the trials of daily living. For this, I can't help but lift my heart in gratitude for Catholicism's spiritual treasures.

13

The Francis Revolution

The first decade of the new millennium seemed to speed by like an old-time silent movie.

The tragic events of September 11, 2001, the wars in Afghanistan and Iraq, the roiling controversies within the church over the clergy abuse crisis, and the financial excesses of the U.S. banking industry and subsequent stock market collapse left little time to reflect upon the lightning pace of our ever-changing world.

The clergy abuse crisis in Boston and other dioceses in the early part of the decade took its emotional toll on many Catholics, including FADICA's members, who maintained commitments in the Catholic world despite their anger over the scandalous behavior of clergy and the concealment of management practices by church leaders.

The collapse of the financial markets in 2008—due mostly to the breakdown in trust within the U.S. financial system caused by subprime mortgage practices and the abuses of derivatives—led to a global recession of historic proportions. Some foundation members in FADICA reported that they were unable to keep donor commitments because of their plummeting endowments.

Like many people in America, I sensed that certain dimensions of my life were not as permanent as I had once assumed.

The aging of our FADICA membership was also taking its toll. Several beloved members died, including Phil Lewis, Greg McCarthy, Tim O'Shaughnessy, George Doty, and Tom Donnelly—all agents of FADICA's remarkable successes over the past few decades. Retirement took others, such as Anthony Brenninkmeyer, a monumental force in our culture of cooperation.

After thirty-three years of leading FADICA, I trusted that the younger members of the various families in our membership would continue the work of their extraordinary parents and grandparents. The organization was in healthy financial shape, thanks to the foresight of its members in solidifying its reserves. After three-plus decades of solid achievement, FADICA had an excellent reputation as an influential force in Catholic philanthropy. It was time for me to pass the leadership of our organization to the next generation.

A search for my successor began. The result was the hiring of an energetic member of the White House Office of Faith-Based Initiatives, Alexia Kelley, a Haverford graduate and former staff member of the USCCB's Catholic Campaign for Human Development. Alexia was known for her past efforts in organizing young Catholic leaders for social justice and environmental action.

I had the satisfaction of knowing that FADICA would be in excellent hands. I retired from the organization with much gratitude for all we had achieved together, the lifelong friendships we had forged, and the deeper understanding of the church's history, its diversity, and the broad sweep of Catholicism's charitable activities. I looked forward to a different pace and a few more years of mentoring and advising in the world of Catholic giving.

The FADICA years showed the power of staying informed and building relationships, as well as the benefits of group collaboration—great lessons for laypeople who desire to help strengthen Catholic life and participate in its mission more fully. As Catholics continue to rise in the ranks of wealth and power, FADICA stands as an important example of continuing one's religious education and impacting the church's life by working with others. As Jesus's parable of the Talents instructs, we cannot return our gifts to the Lord without having shown our entrepreneurial enterprise, and that has been emblematic of this impressive group of caring Christian donors since its inception.

Isaac Newton, defining one of the basic laws of physics, once said, "A body in motion will remain in motion unless it is acted upon by an external force." In other words, things cannot stop or change direction by themselves. That proved true in my own transition. I still had the irrepressible urge to stay involved in the world of church-related charity.

Within weeks of leaving FADICA, I began to set up a consultancy—Drexel Philanthropic Advisors—naming it after the patron saint for philanthropists, Katherine Drexel. Katherine was a member of a banking family who gave up her prominence in Philadelphia society to found a religious order of sisters and later an entire university and system of schools for the underserved. She devoted her inheritance to uplifting the plight of the poor, especially former slaves. Her desire to use wealth for God's service inspired me in counseling donors to achieve maximum impact.

I began working with several foundations and a major international Catholic charity. My days were marked by challenging assignments, from refugee work due to wars in the Middle East to working for the protection of agricultural workers in Latin America. Now freed from the year-to-year administrative tasks that challenge most nonprofit leaders, I was no longer constrained by management duties such as planning conferences and board meetings. I was freer to take part in the increasing number of forums and group discussions on the troubling state of the Catholic Church.

In 2012, intensifying polarization in the church and the burgeoning scandals rocking the Vatican made headlines: the U.S. Catholic bishops were behind an ill-conceived Vatican-led investigation of American sisters to determine their orthodoxy, money laundering at the Vatican bank was being investigated, and the pope's butler leaked documents to an Italian journalist that showed the internal operations at the Holy See as a hotbed of squabbling and corruption.

Then, one year later, Benedict XVI became the first pope to resign since Gregory XII did so in 1415. Demoralized and drained by the intractable problems facing the central administration of the church, Benedict summoned 115 cardinals to Rome to choose his successor. The task for the new pontiff would be to fix the church's scandals and repair the damaged trust.

Few imagined that the ensuing conclave would choose a little-known Jesuit archbishop from Argentina, Jorge Bergoglio. Nor could anyone anticipate that this obscure choice would set in motion a bold new pastoral direction for the church.

It was for many, and certainly for me, a sign of Providence, which is usually more evident when the storm clouds of life gather. A tempest-tossed fishing boat of frightened apostles seemed a good image for Catholicism in those moments. It brought me back to my childhood and the swirling vortex around my father's boat when the manatee rose from underneath us. Dad's wisdom echoed once again: "Be ready for the surprises in life."

Pope Francis was different from the outset. The name he chose was the same as a thirteenth-century preacher who embraced poverty and responded to Christ's call to rebuild his church. The new pontiff's symbolic and reverential bow and request for prayers from the crowds gathered in St. Peter's Square to welcome him on March 13, 2013, was a statement in and of itself. Jesus was to be found in the ordinary lives of people, and Francis seemed to be giving his first homily by reminding fellow clergy and bishops where Christ is located: in the *entire* body of the faithful—a perspective underplayed by clerical mentalities.

Within months, Francis issued his first apostolic exhortation, *The Joy of the Gospel*, which was a framework for his papacy and a revolutionary shift of emphasis to the good news of the merciful, forgiving, healing God. He introduced his image of the Catholic Church as a "field hospital" during a battle, where people were wounded or dying and needed compassion, not harsh judgment.

Francis was determined to challenge those many bishops who see the church as a self-protecting fortress. A clericalized church so accustomed to deploying moral teachings as weapons against its people and the world was destroying Catholicism's more gospel-like image as a community of love and mercy.

With Pope Francis, it was time for more listening, praying, and accepting the unruly freedom of God's word, alive even in the most complicated circumstances of human living. For him, the appropriate Christian ministry is one of "accompaniment." His vision, inspired by the Second Vatican Council, envisages an active, participative church in which the entire people of God are engaged in proclaiming the good news of the Christian gospel through actions more than words.

Each day of Francis's pontificate has brought hope to rank-and-file Catholics, who turned out in droves to see Francis both in Rome and during a series of papal visits across the globe.

Decades of seeing the appointment of bishops who reacted against the dynamic of renewal set forth by the Second Vatican Council, combined with daily revelations about clergy abuse scandals, had worn down the faithful. The result was unprecedented declines in church practice and a catastrophic drop in vocations in the United States and Europe.

Pope Francis, seen mostly smiling, humbly carrying his own baggage, living in simple quarters with a community of people, driving around in a small Fiat, delivering daily spiritual reflections on the loving essence of the gospel, seemed like a pope who had been dreamed up by movie screenwriters.

The new pope wasted little time replacing the Vatican's secretary of state and other high-ranking officials in Rome. He put in place a handpicked cabinet of cardinals to advise him and placed the finances of the Holy See on a more accountable course by introducing stronger financial controls.

As the months progressed, the *New York Times* and other world dailies provided saturation coverage of Francis's words, travels, and actions. And while many wondered how long the new pontiff would be around, inasmuch as he was entering his eighties, it was becoming clear that change and improvement in the church had a good chance of gaining momentum.

Yet resistance to this change proved formidable.

In the fall of 2014, two years into his papacy, Francis came to the United States. The unhappiness of those prelates feeling the sting of Francis's initial purges began to be evident. Despite the crowded streets of well-wishers and the thunderous applause of political leaders, the pope's visit was met by the restrained attentiveness of prominent U.S. Catholic archbishops. An awkward scheme by the U.S. papal nuncio, Archbishop Carlo Maria Viganò, to enlist Francis's influence in a conservative political battle over gay marriage marred the papal tour. Viganò invited Kimberly Davis, a Kentucky county clerk, to meet the pope at the Vatican's U.S. Embassy. At the time, Davis had been held in contempt of a federal court order for refusing to issue a marriage license to same-sex couples because of her own personal religious objections.

The pope was not pleased to be thrust into the middle of a highly fractious American debate. Nevertheless, there was extensive press coverage on the Davis meeting, which detracted from the overall positive aspects of the papal visit.

The Vatican's public statements clarified that the Embassy episode involving the Pope was not to be understood as support for Davis's actions. Even so, the mishap that Viganò had arranged left the pope feeling unfairly manipulated at a time when he was challenging the church to be more welcoming and less judgmental of gay people.

Consequently, Archbishop Viganò was called back to the Vatican. The botched attempt to embarrass the pope meant no further career advancement for the former nuncio. That, in turn, stoked the fires of retribution by Viganò that we would come to understand later.

Still, the uneasiness of the U.S. church hierarchy with Pope Francis grew even more noticeable in 2015 as the international synod of bishops convened in Rome to discuss the subjects of marriage and the family.

Pope Francis's call for a more innovative, less legalistic pastoral approach to Catholics who divorce, remarry, and seek readmission to the church and reception of the Eucharist sparked bold, open attacks on him. One prominent American cardinal carried on a public campaign that questioned Francis's orthodoxy.

Pope Francis's overarching concern, however, was connecting again with people whose lives fell short of the ideal of Christian practice. He appealed to his critics' punctilious and legalistic approach with a reminder of those moments in their own lives when mercy and forgiveness made a powerful transformative difference.

For bishops inclined to police their flocks for deviations from exacting formulations of doctrine, moral practices, and church law, Francis's new, more pastoral attitude appeared dangerously compromising.

For those of us who had experienced many aspects of the rigidity and clericalism that Francis was fighting, his new approach was long overdue.

For decades, many church leaders had operated as though their job was to protect a medieval fortress from the onslaught of sinful and heretical hordes. Over time, monitoring compliance with rules formed the core task of bishops. One's ecclesiastical career was advanced by scrupulous enforcement of doctrinal formulations and rules rather than through reputations for pastoral sensitivity or building supportive, loving relationships within the Catholic flock.

Now Pope Francis was returning the Christian community to its core mission of mercy and love, describing the church as a people accompanying one another through the challenges of life.

Like millions of Catholics, I welcomed this direction. The church as a community has always been a compelling aspect for me. So many within this community have drawn me more deeply into its life—my family, Catholic school teachers, seminary faculty, coworkers at the bishops' conference, Catholic philanthropists, and fellow parishioners. I considered the church a place of welcome that nourished my spiritual hunger and provided friendship, affirmation, and learning—a community that inspired generosity and compassion. Creeds and rules had their place, but the church's true power was beyond its sometimes too abstract formulations and pronouncement of its hierarchy and priests. It lay in scaled gatherings of its members reflecting an inclusive, loving presence of its founder, or a common mission of service—the hallmark of the church.

Pope Francis invited the faithful to a deeper understanding of their Christian identity more along these lines.

Yet the elements of a titanic battle over the direction of the church under Francis's leadership continued to fall into place. It would take only an incident to set off an explosion of brewing discontent among the forces of opposition. This moment arrived in June 2018, with the scandalous revelations about the retired American and now-former cardinal Theodore McCarrick.

Francis had disciplined McCarrick following an investigation by the Archdiocese of New York into the molestation of a former altar server and rumors of the former cardinal's abuse of seminarians. Public outrage erupted over the revelations. Reactionary forces used the incident to rally behind the former U.S. nuncio, Archbishop Viganò, who charged in a public letter published in a conservative U.S. Catholic newspaper that Pope Francis and the Vatican had ignored warnings about McCarrick.

In truth, the rise of McCarrick within the church had more to do with the decisions of pontiffs prior to Francis. Yet Francis remained silent before Viganò's charges, convinced that over time Viganò's claims would be seen as baseless.

Battles with conservative forces notwithstanding, Francis did not seem to grasp fully the depth of public discontent over the case of Theodore McCarrick. It marked an entirely new chapter for Francis's papacy, leaving veteran observers like myself wondering what the church might look like if changes were not made and made quickly.

14

Back to the Future

The scandal involving Theodore McCarrick marked an entirely new chapter for the Catholic Church. It was likened to the era of the Reformation in the sixteenth century when an Augustinian monk, Martin Luther, publicly excoriated the pope for selling indulgences and reprieves from penance.

The comparison to this historic split in Christianity with the present scandals befalling the Catholic hierarchy epitomized in the case of McCarrick marked a watershed moment for Catholicism sure to indicate the closing of one era and the opening of a new one.

Suddenly, it seemed that average parishioners had reached the breaking point. The Gallup polling organization reported that one in four Catholics had little or no confidence in priests or bishops. Over a third of Catholics were now questioning whether they would remain in the church—an increase of some fifteen percentage points from the 2002 scandals of the Boston archdiocese.

Prominent Catholic universities and nonprofit organizations held well-attended conferences about the McCarrick case and what it revealed about the colossal corruption and lack of accountability in the church.

State legislatures extended deadlines for clergy-victim lawsuits, and attorneys general probed chancery records for evidence of criminal behavior and cover-up by dioceses stretching back decades.

The moment seemed surreal and weighed heavily on many

Catholics confronted daily with hurtful revelations about the state of the church that had been at the center of their lives.

In Washington, DC—ground zero for the McCarrick scandal—the archdiocese functioned without a full-time archbishop. Its newly retired archbishop, Cardinal Donald Wuerl, was virtually invisible after first telling the public that he had no knowledge of his predecessor McCarrick's wrongdoing, and then when facts proved otherwise, he sheepishly explained that he had forgotten.

Within my own Jesuit parish, Holy Trinity, our conscientious pastor, Kevin Gillespie, SJ, conducted parish forums and small group discussions, giving parishioners a chance to air their emotions and channel their grief into plans of action.

The McCarrick case seemed to be the straw that had broken the camel's back. The abysmal church leadership that victimized so many and the clerical wall of secrecy would no longer be tolerated.

Instead, the solidly loyal faithful were demanding change—not only in the way the hierarchy was chosen, but in a structure that allowed the ordained to govern and dominate while the faithful in the pews were relegated to listen and submit in unquestioning obedience.

It was now becoming clear to many Catholics that this arrangement played a role in the massive cover-up and inaction on clergy sexual abuse.

More than a few lay Catholics were familiar with the church's constitutional documents set forth in the reform-oriented Second Vatican Council. They realized that the implementation of fundamental principles that council members articulated had been stymied in their implementation by bishops fearful of the loss of power. A great wall of separation between clergy and laypeople had been reinforced, leaving the council's call for a communitarian framework unfulfilled.

The historic council had laid out an understanding of church membership based on the dignity conferred on each member by virtue of their baptism. Any functions and distinctions from thereon were secondary to this basic reality—the equality and calling of each baptized member of the community to constitute one people.

As lay Catholics continued to deepen their understanding of the church's present state, more and more issues about its daily life surfaced: declining Mass attendance; the loss of younger Catholics; the exclusion of women from the clergy; the accelerating inability of dioceses to find priests for their parishes; the precipitous decline of parochial schools; and of course, looming in the headlines, the abuse of children by priests and those serving in the church's higher offices.

With the McCarrick crisis driving Catholic anger and state officeholders feeling pressures to take action, the U.S. Catholic bishops attempted to introduce new accountability practices that would make greater use of law enforcement and third parties to investigate future cases of sexual abuse or diocesan cover-ups.

Pope Francis called together a worldwide synod of bishops on the sexual abuse in February 2019, but its proceedings fell short of expectations and specific measures signaling that the church globally was ready for serious accountability and uniform zero toleration at all levels.

In the United States, bishops announced the probable adoption of a plan of reporting abuse to an independent lay panel and greater legal powers to report and discipline bishops who have mishandled sexual abuse in their dioceses.

While all of this was to be decided by bishops, other countries like Germany took a new approach and announced a council of clergy and laity and a listening process that sounded remarkably familiar to me.

Cardinal Gerhard Marx of Berlin, during a press conference in March 2019 announcing the German Catholic plan of action in his country, stated, "The church can only grow and deepen if we are liberated from blocked thinking in order to pursue free and open debates and show the ability to take new positions and go down new paths."

I was sitting at my desk reading the story of the German cardinal's news conference and turned to look up at a nearby bookshelf where I kept a photograph of Cardinal John Dearden taken during the Call to Action conference.

Dearden's face seemed to be noticeably more blissful this day, as though he were sending a message through time that was saying, "I told you, we'd get there someday." He had confided in me during the Detroit event in 1976, "We may be seeing now something like our way of proceeding in the future."

Four decades ago, at the Call to Action conference, Cardinal Dearden had opened that meeting of over a thousand U.S. Catholic laypeople, clergy, and bishops, many of whom had been elected to represent their dioceses to help enact a plan of action for the church.

Before the conference had gotten under way, Dearden summed up what was most significant in the long process of listening and preparation for that day in the testimonies of thousands of Catholics: "They urged all Catholics to work together to make the church a more fitting witness to the truths which it proclaims."

As the German bishops moved forward with an extensive process not dissimilar to the Call to Action, and as bishops in other countries began to explore newer, more inclusive ways of exploring urgently needed reforms, I was struck by the fact that the church has come full circle.

I wondered what kind of church we might have had if ecclesiastical ambition and fear of change had not sidetracked Dearden's experiment forty-three years ago.

Would the secrecy and malfeasance of the clergy abuse scandal have been uncovered much earlier? Would McCarrick's advancement have been possible especially after Call to Action decades before had demanded that the local church be involved in the selection of bishops and pastors? Would we have seen the attrition, division, and erosion of trust had there been more direct and transparent communication in the church? The questions keep emerging.

What I do know now is that the unaccountable and exclusionary way that Catholic leaders in this country have operated is giving way to a new chapter in which the influence of all its members will be measurably more evident.

When the history of this transitional era is written, it may not pinpoint the time when the church began to function with greater voice and engagement of all of its members. Nonetheless, the forces for change will have had their roots in Catholic parishes and in the lives of individual believers, lay and clergy alike, who throughout the divisions and scandals that have marked the history of the Catholic Church these last decades did not give up hope and heroically cared enough to insist on change.

15

Joined as One Community

Amid almost weekly headlines focused on some aspect of the Catholic Church's predicaments, Fran and I drove to southern Virginia for the baptism of our sixth grandchild, Eleanor. It was a beautiful sunny Sunday as the family gathered in Norfolk for this special occasion.

Our son John, and his wife, Kate, had settled in that city during John's last posting as an active-duty naval officer. They lived in Norfolk's Ghent neighborhood with its century-old homes near historic Mowbray Arch and its glorious view of the Elizabeth River.

Fran and I felt blessed that our children practiced their faith and were so supportive of one another at important moments like this. Today, we would initiate a new member of our family into our Catholic community. We rejoiced at the thought of the gospel choir at John and Kate's parish, St. Mary's Basilica, a mile from their home.

St. Mary's was built in the mid-nineteenth century. During recent decades, it has housed a primarily African American membership known for its inspirational music and warm hospitality. Lately, it has experienced a surge in membership, due in large part to the powerful preaching of its Irish American pastor, Fr. Jim Curran.

Our family, along with Kate's, took up the two front pews. We clapped and sang the entrance song, "Soon and Very Soon," while Fr. Jim, a deacon, and other ministers, women and men—African American and white—moved toward the sanctuary, waving and smiling broadly to those gathered. The warm, joyful spirit radiating from fellow worshipers, Fr. Jim's exceptional preaching, and our gathered family proved a potent emotional combination.

After the homily, our family was invited to the sanctuary where baby Eleanor was baptized before the smiling faces of her parents, grandparents, sister, cousins, aunts, and uncles, while the choir and musicians looked on with glad approval. Our daughter Meghan and her husband, Ricardo, were godparents. Our daughter Ellen and her husband, James, and all of our granchildren, were also there.

Each of us traced the cross on Eleanor's forehead. Fr. Jim hoisted baby Eleanor above his head to receive the congregation's loud applause. I experienced sheer joy as Eleanor's parents carried their newly baptized infant daughter up and down St. Mary's aisles while parishioners reached out to bless Eleanor. This was a loving St. Mary's traditional welcome.

It was an experience of Catholicism that captured for me the church's glorious power to connect people with Christ and to feel his love, joined as one community, the body of Christ.

Eleanor's baptism at the historic Basilica of St. Mary's, Norfolk, Virginia

Words failed me. It was something to experience and to marvel at, the moment penetrating the deepest regions of my heart. I love Catholicism and the amazing and mysterious journey I have taken under its light. I want more than anything for my progeny to experience this too. My prayer for my granddaughter was that she anticipate what God's remarkable grace has in store for her life, and that God's people, who gather around church altars, like the one at St. Mary's, would, by their prayers and kindness, continue to mirror God's love and support for her throughout her journey.

Life's uncertainties were suspended in those precious moments at Eleanor's baptism. The relentless questioning of my days seemed unimportant in this scene of peace and the blessing of the congregation.

We clutter our lives with concerns that prove over time to be of passing consequence. Even as believers, we give too much space and too much time to abstractions, propositions, and partisan wrangling, and not enough time for absorbing God's unconditional care for us and for reflecting on the grace of belonging to one another on this human journey. Yet this can be keenly felt in moments like this; of joining with others to celebrate and give praise.

As I looked down on the blissful face of our newly baptized granddaughter, I thought of the grace of my Catholic journey over the past seven decades. I breathed in an intense gladness. Eleanor, too, was now on the life-giving trajectory of faith that, like my own, enriches everything encountered in this world.

I am grateful that this story continues through the lives of those who, like Eleanor, we welcome into this great faith. May they and all who have shared this story come to know the treasure of the Catholic community—its enduring witness to the gospel, its prayer, sacraments, and loving service. These have been, for this glad traveler, the dazzling blessings of belonging.

Index

Page numbers in italics refer to photos.

101st Airborne (U.S. Army), 4
9/11, 160
accompaniment (Pope Francis),
   163–64
Affordable Care Act (ACA), 55
Afghanistan, 160
Alexandria Gazette, 1
Alexandria, VA, 1
Alliance for Catholic Education
   (ACE), 148
America magazine, 136–37
Anglicanism, 50
Ann (sister), 12
Apostolicam actuositatem, x
APSA (Administration of the
   Patrimony of the Apostolic
   See), 115
Aristotle, 37
Assateague Island, MD, 40, 41
Assisi, Italy, 155
autonomy, diocesan, 60

Baltakis, Paulius, OFM (bishop),
   123, 125
Banco Ambrosiano, 98–100
bankruptcy, diocesan, 136
Barbara (sister), 12
Bardstown, KY, 156
Baroni, Geno, 80
Barre, Tom, *28*
Basilica of St. Clement (Rome),
   153–54

Basilica of St. Francis (Assisi,
   Italy), 155
Basilica of St. Mary (Norfolk, VA),
   173–75, *174*
Basilica of St. Peter (Rome), 154
Battle of the Bulge, 4
Baum, William (cardinal), 61, 71,
   73
beatnik culture, 48
Belfast, 155
belonging, 173–75
Benedict XVI (pope), xvi, 162
Bennett, Robert, 132–33
Bergoglio, Jorge, SJ. *See* Francis
   (pope)
Berlin Wall, 120
Bernardin, Joseph L. (cardinal), 60,
   70–75, 77, 122, 124, *125*
Berry, Jason, 129
Berry, John, 20
Big Sur, CA, 48
Blessed Sacrament Catholic
   Church (Alexandria, VA), 2,
   144
Bob and Delores Hope Founda-
   tion, 88–89
Boileau, David, 34–35
Boisi, Geoffrey, 137–43
Book Cadillac Hotel (Detroit), 69
Boston, Archdiocese of, 129–31,
   160, 168
Boston College, 137, 158
Boston Globe, 129–31, 134, 138
Bread for the World, 95

Brencanda Foundation, 82, 90, 102
Brenninkmeyer, Anthony, 90–92,
    96, 113, 115, *117*, 161
Briggs, Kenneth, 64
Brooks, David, xiii
Brown Brothers Harriman & Co.,
    81
Brown v. Board of Education, 24
Bruderman, John, 81–82, 86
Burns (priest), 15–16
Butler, Al (father), 1–2, 5–6, 7–8,
    10–11, 12, 14–15, 41, 163
Butler, Alby (brother), 2, 6, 10, 16,
    131–32
Butler, Dick (brother), 2, 11
Butler, Fran (née Farrell)
    and CUA, 40, 41, 45, 130
    family life, 47–49, 50, 56–57, 173
    growing relationship with, 45–47
    marriage, 47
    idea for Call to Action hearings,
        61
    travels with, 152–53, 155
    walks along beach with, 40,
        41–43, *43*
    work at U.S. Senate, 49, 51, 61
Butler, Jean (mother), 1–2, 6,
    12–13, 15–16, 39, 40–41
Butler, John (son), 50, 173
Butler, Tom (brother), 1, 2, 11
Byron, William J., SJ, 95
Byzantine Rite. *See* Ukrainian
    Greek Catholic Church

Cafferty, Margaret, PVBM, 67, 69
Call to Action. See Octogesima adveniens
    (Pope Paul VI)
Call to Action conference, x, xi,
    xiii, 66, 69–70, 170–71
Call to Action hearings, 61–66, *63*,
    64, *65*
canon law, 134
Cape Canaveral, FL, xi, 8, 13

Caprio, Giuseppe (cardinal), 100
CARA (Center for Applied
    Research in the Apostolate),
    80–81
Carberry, John (cardinal), 71, 72
Carmody, Charles, 6
Carrie Estelle Doheny Foundation,
    86–87, 88
Carr, John, 68, *123*
Cassidy, Sheila, 64
Cassin, B. J., 147
Castelli, Jim, 107
Cathedral of St. George (Lviv), 126
Cather, Willa, ix
Catholic Campaign for Human
    Development (USCCB), 161
Catholic Charities, 55, 61, 67, 68,
    69
Catholic Church Extension Society,
    97
Catholic Committee on Urban
    Ministry (CCUM), 67
Catholic culture, 5, 9, 150
Catholic hospitals. *See* health care,
    Catholic (two words in the
    text and MW Dict.)
Catholic Near East Welfare Asso-
    ciation (CNEWA), 123, 152
Catholic schools. *See* education,
    Catholic
Catholic social teaching, 55–56,
    77, 106
Catholic Telecommunications Net-
    work of America (CTNA),
    113
Catholic University of America, xi,
    37, 40–41, 43–47, 48, 57, 61,
    95, 107, 145, 130
Catholic Worker movement, 64
Catholic Youth Organization
    (CYO), 54
Central High School (Little Rock,
    AR), 24

Charter for the Protection of Children and Young People (USCCB), 132

Chavez, Cesar, *64*

Chicago Daily News, 60

Christo Rey Jesuit High School (Chicago), 147

Christo Rey movement, 147–49

Christ, the Light of the World (Kommendi), 52

church history, 151–59

Church of the Gate (Vilnius, Lithuania), 124

Church of the Holy Sepulcher (Jerusalem), 152

Cingolani, Bill, *28*

Circus of Nero (Rome), 154

City Connects (Boston College), 149

Civil Rights Act, 64

Civil Rights movement, 27. *See also* Jim Crow; segregation

clergy abuse crisis, 129–43, 144, 160, 168–72

financial dimensions of, 133–34

clericalism, 44, 163, 166

Clinton Administration, 61

Cocoa Beach, FL, xi, 13–14

Cold War, 4

Collège de la Sainte Famille (Cairo), 91, 92 (Referred to by the English translation.)

College of New Rochelle (New Rochelle, NY), 67

College of Notre Dame (Baltimore), 109

College of the Holy Cross (Worcester, MA), 67, 147

colonialism, 35

Committee for National Health Insurance (CNHI), 55

Committee for Communications (USCC), 69, 73

Committee for the Catholic Observance of the Bicentennial (NCCB), 59–71

Committee on Social Development (USCC), 121

communism, 4, 36, 120

Congregation for the Evangelization of Peoples, 99, 120

Congregation for the Propagation of the Faith. *See* Congregation for the Evangelization of Peoples

Conrad N. Hilton Foundation, 89–90, 96, 105

Constantine, 153, 154

Corporation for National Service (CNS), 148

cosmology, 33–34

Cotter, Bill, 49

Cotter, Carole, 49

Cranston, Senator Alan, 49

CTNA. *See* Catholic Telecommunications Network of America (CTNA)

CUA. *See* Catholic University of America

Cunningham, Lawrence S., 156–57

Curran, Charles E., 41

Curran, James, 173–74

Cushing, Richard J. (cardinal), 68, 80

Dallas Charter. *See* Charter for the Protection of Children and Young People (USCCB)

Davis, Kimberly, 165

Day, Dorothy, 64, *65*

Dearden, John (cardinal)

Bicentennial Committee, x, 57, 59, 60, *63*, 170–71

post–Call to Action fallout, 70–71, 73–74, 77, 78,

vision of laity and clergy, 81

Death Comes to the Archbishop (Cather), ix

DeCastro, Dale, *28*

DePaul University College of Law, 97

DeRance Foundation, 82–86

Descartes, René, 37

Dessommes, Larry, *28*

Detroit Athletic Club, 113

discernment, vocational, 44

divorced Catholics, 63, 76

Doheny, Edward, 87

Doheny Foundation. *See* Carrie Estelle Doheny Foundation

Domestic Policy Office (USCC), 65–66, 68, 71

Donnelly Foundation. *See* Mary J. Donnelly Foundation

Donnelly, Mary J., 95

Donnelly, Thomas J., 95–96, 100–101, 113, 115, 130, 160

Doty, George Espy, 92–95, 96, 113–15, 160

Drane, James F., 21, 25

Drexel Philanthropic Advisors, 162

Drexel, St. Katherine, 162

Dublin, 156

Dulles, Avery, SJ (cardinal), 61

Dupont Chemical Company, 93

Dupont Circle (Washington, DC), 134

Economic Justice for All (NCCB), 106, 108

Economic Prefecture. *See* Prefecture for the Economic Affairs of the Holy See

education, Catholic, 4–5, 142, 144–50

Egan, Jack, 67

Eleanor (grandchild), 173–75, *174*

Ellen (daughter), 50, 148–49, 174

Embassy Row (Washington, DC), 112

Empire State Building, 93

episcopal appointments, 139–40

Erath, LA, 27–28

Evangelii Gaudium (Pope Francis), 163

Excelsior Hotel (Rome), 99

FADICA (Foundations and Donors Interested in Catholic Activities)

and Catholic schools, 146

clergy abuse scandal, 131, 134–37, 156

FB's early work with, 80–101

FB's hire, 80–82

FB's retirement, 79, 161, 162

members, 82–101, 160

Santa Fe meeting, ix–x, 158

trips, 120, 122–28, 151–58

work of, xi

Fahey, Charles J., 102

Fall, Senator Albert B., 87

family, 1–4, 6–8, 42–43, 173–75

Farmer, James Leonard, Jr., 46

Farmers Home Insurance Company, 87

Farrell family (in-laws), 42–43

Faubus, Orval, 24

FBI (Federal Bureau of Investigation), 133

Federated Investors, 95

Fernandez, Geno, 142–43

Fialka, John J., 102, 107–11,

Finance Committee (USCC), 104

financial stewardship, 136

financial transparency. *See* transparency, financial

First Vatican Council. *See* Vatican I Council

Fitzgerald, Bishop Edward, 19

Fletcher, Bishop Albert L., 35, 38

Foley, John Patrick (cardinal), 100

Foley, John, SJ, 146–47

Fordham University, 92, 93, 102

Fort Hunt Park (Fort Hunt, VA), 56
Francis (pope), xiii, xvi, 44, 118,
    155, 157, 163–67, 170
Frank (uncle), 4
fundraising, 121

Galilei, Galileo, 33–34
Gallagher, Donald, 82, 85
Gallagher, Idella, 82
Gallin, Alice, OSU, 67
Gallup, 136, 168
Gauthe, Gilbert, 129
gay rights, 63, 76, 165
General Electric, 92, 131
General Motors, 93
Geoghan, John, 129–30
George, Francis, OMI (cardinal),
    140–41
Georgetown University, 87, 107,
    148, 157, 158
Gerety, Peter Leo (archbishop), *63*
Gethsemani, Abbey of (Bard-
    stown, KY), 156–57
Ghent (Norfolk, VA), 173
GI Bill (Servicemen's Readjustment
    Act of 1944), 4
Gillespie, Kevin, SJ, 169
Glendalough Abbey, 156
Goldman Sachs, 92, 139
Gorbachev, Mikhail, 124
Grace, Charles M., 89
Grace, J. Peter, Jr., 89
Gray, Howard J., SJ, 157–58
Great Society, 51
Greeley, Andrew M., 60–61, 62–63,
    69
Gregory XII (pope), 162
Griffin, John Howard, 26
Griffiths, Martha, 55
Groundhog Day (film), 113
Gudziak, Borys, 126

Harding Administration, 87
Hattler, Denise, 106, 111

Haverford College, 161
Healey, Thomas J., 139–40
health care, Catholic, 51, 52–55
Hehir, J. Bryan, 68, 73
Heidegger, Martin, 37
Hemrick, Eugene F., 107
Herald American (Chicago), 70
Herman, Alexis, 61
Hesburgh, Theodore, CSC
hierarchy, distrust of, 32–33, 35
Higgins, George G., 53, 55, 62–63,
    63
Hilton, Conrad N., 90
Hilton Foundation. *See* Conrad N.
    Hilton Foundation
Himes, Michael, 158
hippie culture, 48
Holy Family School (Cairo). *See*
    Collège de la Sainte Famille
    (Cairo) (*Referred to as Holy
    Family School in the text)
Holy See (Vatican), 72, 79, 98–101,
    112–18, 120, 122, 153–54,
    162, 165, 167
Holy Trinity Catholic Church
    (Washington, DC), xv, 169
Hope, Delores, 89
Hope Foundation. *See* Bob and
    Delores Hope Foundation
hospitals. *See* health care, Catholic
Houghton, Rosemary, 158
Hoye, Daniel, 104–5, 109
Hubbs, Donald H., 89–90
Hudon, Mary Oliver, SND, 109
Hughes, Alfred C. (archbishop),
    142
Hurley, Joseph (archbishop), 37
Hurricane Andrew, 142
Hurricane Katrina, 142–43

Ignatius of Loyola, Saint, xii, 158
immigration, 4, 31, 62, 145
Inquisition, 33
Institute for Religious Works. *See*

IOR (Institute for Religious Works)

Institute of Church History. *See* Ukrainian Catholic University

integration. *See* segregation

Inter Insignores (Paul VI), 72

International Eucharistic Congress, 41st (Philadelphia), 59–60, 72

Invisible Man (Ellison), 25

IOR (Institute for the Works of Religion), 98–99, 100, 118

Iraq, 160

Ireland, Republic of, xvi, 151, 56

Irish Republican Army, 2

Iron Gate Inn (Washington, DC), 107

Israel, State of, 151–53

Jadot, Jean (archbishop), 70

James (son-in-law), 174

Jaspers, Karl, 37

Jefferson Airplane, 48

Jesuits. *See* Society of Jesus

Jesus del Monte, Michoacán, Mexico, 32

Jim Crow, 28

John, Erica P., 82, 85, 86, 113, 115

John, Harry G., Jr., 82–86

John Paul II Cultural Center (Washington, DC), 137

John Paul II (pope), 75, 81, 85, 101, 112, 113, 114, 115, *117*, 118, 120

Johnson, Lyndon, 51

Joy of the Gospel, The. *See Evangelii Gaudium* (Pope Francis)

justice. *See* social justice

Kate (daughter-in-law), 173

Keating, Thomas, OCSO, 158

Kelley, Alexia, 161

Kelley, Tom, 20

Kelly, Thomas, OP (archbishop), 72–73

Kennedy, John, xi, 26–27

Kennedy, Robert, xi, 46

Kennedy, Ted, 55

Kierkegaard, Søren, 37

King, Martin Luther, Jr., xi, 45

Knights of Columbus, 5

Kommendi, Eugene, 52

Krol, John (cardinal), 59–60, 71–72

L'Arche Daybreak (Toronto), 157

Lafayette, Diocese of, 129

Laghi, Pio (cardinal), 112–13

laity, role of, 45, 50, 59, 60, 96, 98, 143, 170

Lake Charles, Diocese of, 149

Lake Tahoe, 48

Lakewood (Cleveland, OH), 3

Lally, Francis J., 68, 72

Lamy, Jean-Baptiste (archbishop), ix

Lara, Rosalio Jose Castillo, SDB (cardinal), 115–18

Lateran Palace (Rome), 153

Law, Bernard Francis (cardinal), 129–31

Leadership Roundtable, 141–43

Learning to Serve (Carmody), 6–7

Leavey, Dorothy E. Risley, 87

Leavey Foundation. *See* Thomas and Dorothy Leavey Foundation

Leavey, Thomas E., 87

Ledbetter, Calvin, Jr., 35

Levada, William Joseph (cardinal), 138

Lewis, Edward D., 96

Lewis, Frank J., 96–97

Lewis, Philip D., 96–98, 160

Lewis University, 97

liberation theology, 58

Linders, Bert, SJ, 91–92, 93

Little Rock, AR, 24–27, 38–39
Little Rock, Diocese of, 19
Little Village (Chicago), 147
Losten, Basil H. (bishop), *123*
Loyola Foundation, 106, 111
Loyola University New Orleans, 38
Lumen Gentium (Vatican II), xiii, 74
Luther, Martin, 168
Lynch, Robert Nugent (bishop),
    121, 122
Lviv, Ukraine, 126

Mahoney, Charlotte, 68
Mahony, Roger M. (cardinal),
    121–22
Makeska, David, *28*
Malone, James William (bishop),
    94–95
management, church, 113–19, 144
Manchino, John, *28*
Manhattanville College, 106
Marcel, Gabriel, 37
March on Washington (1963), 64
Marcinkus, Paul (archbishop), 99
Markusen, Ann, 42
Marquette University, 82
marriage, 47
married clergy, 76, 127
Martin, James, SJ, ix–xiii, 158
Marx, Gerhard (cardinal), 170
Mary J. Donnelly Foundation, 96
Mayflower Hotel (Washington,
    DC), 81, 110
May, John L. (archbishop), *123*, 127
McCarrick, Theodore, xv–xvi, 167,
    168–71
McCarthy, Gregory, III, 160
McCarthy, J. Thomas, 88
McChesney, Kathleen, 133, 135
McGann, John R. (bishop), 104
McKinless, Kathleen, 134
McKinsey & Co., 142
McNicholas, Joseph A. (bishop), 72

Medellín Conference, 57–58
Medicare/Medicaid, 51
Meghan (daughter), 50, 174
Meehan, Terrance, 89
Melczek, Dale J. (bishop), 140
Mellon, Catherine, 58
Merrill Lynch & Co., 114
Merton, Thomas, OCSO, 156–57
Microsoft, 92
Middlebury College, 21
Military Air Transport Service
    (MATS), 1
Miller Brewing Company, 82
Miller, Frederick, 82
Millionaire, The (TV series), 83
Mindszenty, József (cardinal), 4
Mlocek, Frances, IHM, 103–4
    (Check that spelling in text
    "Mlocek" is correct)
Monan, J. Donald, SJ, 137, 140
Mondale, Walter, 64
Montessori, Maria, 15
Montreal, 47
moral teaching, 34. *See also* Catholic
    social teaching
Morelia, Michoacán, Mexico, 28, 29
Mugovero, Francis John (bishop),
    63
Mullen, Andy, CP, 7–8

NAACP, 24
Nancy (neighbor), 49
Narragansett Bay, 42
National Bicentennial Conference.
    See Call to Action Conference
National Catholic Conference of
    Bishops (NCCB), x, 59, 61–
    62, 70, 72–75, 77–78. *See also*
    Committee for the Catholic
    Observance of the Bicenten-
    nial (NCCB); *Economic Justice
    for All* (NCCB); "To Do the
    Work of Justice" (NCCB)

National Catholic Register, 85

National Catholic Reporter, 62, 129

National Catholic Welfare Conference (NCWC), 51

National Center for Urban and Ethnic Affairs, 80

National Conference of Catholic Women (NCCW), 54

National Guard, 46

National Leadership Roundtable on Church Management. *See* Leadership Roundtable

National Religious Retirement Office (USCC/USCCB), 105, 106, 109, 111

National Review Board, 132. *See also* Charter for the Protection of Children and Young People (USCCB)

NCCB. *See* National Catholic Conference of Bishops (NCCB)

New Madrid Fault Line, 23

New Orleans, Archdiocese of, 142–43

New York, Archdiocese of, 167

New York Stock Exchange (NYSE), 92

New York Times, 64, 164

Newman, Saint John Henry, 50, 51

Newton, Sir Isaac, 161–62

Nixon Administration, 58

Noel (neighbor), 49

Northern Ireland, 155–56

Northwestern University, 35

Notre Dame. *See* University of Notre Dame

Nouwen, Henri, 157

Novak, Michael, 60–61

O'Brien, David J., 67–68

O'Connell, James, 34

O'Shaughnessy, Timothy J., 160

Oakley, Francis, 136

Octogesima adveniens (Paul VI), 66

Office for Child Protection (USCCB), 132–33, 135. *See also* Charter for the Protection of Children and Young People (USCCB); National Review Board

Office for Health and Hospitals (USCC), 54–56, 58–59

Official Catholic Directory (*ODC*), 82

Our Lady of Lourdes Catholic Church (Erath, LA), 27–28

Our Lady of Lourdes Catholic School (Melbourne, FL), 8–9, 13, 67, 144, 152

Our Lady of the Angels Cathedral (Los Angeles), 121

Palmer House Hotel (Chicago), 74

parenthood, 50

Parks, Rosa, 24

Patrick Air Force Base, 5, 7, 14

Paul VI (pope), 66, 70, 114

Pennington, Basil, OCSO, 158

Pennsylvania Diocese Victims Report, xvi

Pentagon, 1, 8

Perot, Ross, 110

Pew Research Center, xii

philanthropy, 79–101, 146

philosophy, 37

Pike, James (bishop), 34–35

Pilarczyk, Daniel (archbishop), 122

pilgrimage, 151–59

Pilot (Boston), 68

Pilsen (Chicago), 147

Pinkerton Security, 47

Pius IX (pope), 18

plate tectonics, 23–24

Plato, 37

polarization, 162

Pontifical Commission for Social Communications, 100